# THE COLLABORATION

## OF

# WEBSTER AND DEKKER

by

Frederick Erastus Pierce

ARCHON BOOKS
1972

Library of Congress Cataloging in Publication Data

Pierce, Frederick Erastus, 1878-1935.
    The collaboration of Webster and Dekker.

    Reprint of the 1909 ed., which was issued as v. 37 of
Yale studies in English.
    Originally presented as the author's thesis, Yale, 1908.
    1. Webster, John, 1580?-1625? 2. Dekker, Thomas,
1570?-1641? I. Title. II. Series: Yale studies in English,
v. 37.
PR3187.P5 1972            822'.3'09            72-6869
ISBN 0-208-01134-X

First published 1909
Reprinted 1972 with permission of
Yale University Press
in an unaltered and unabridged edition
as an Archon Book
by The Shoe String Press, Inc.,
Hamden, Connecticut 06514

[Yale Studies in English, vol. 37]

*Printed in the United States of America*

# PREFACE.

The man who examines problems of collaboration faces a double danger. In the first place, there is always the possibility that all his labors may fail to convince any one but himself. In the second place, there is the risk that so much close and mechanical application may crush out the finer qualities of his own literary nature. I cannot claim to have avoided wholly either of these pitfalls; nevertheless, after all the chaff has been sifted away from this little treatise, I hope that there may still be found a small residuum of wheat, as some definite addition to the world of knowledge; and I also hope that my readers will peruse this book in the same spirit in which it was written—not as a piece of hackwork, but as a sympathetic, although necessarily accurate, study of two great poets. The collaborated plays of Beaumont and Fletcher stand as the monument of one of the most beautiful of human friendships. The collaborated plays of Webster and Dekker form a more humble memorial of what was probably a shoulder-to-shoulder alliance in their pitiful warfare against lifelong poverty. No apology is needed for attempting to throw light on such a partnership.

I wish to express my sincere thanks to Professor Albert S. Cook and to the other members of the English Faculty at Yale for the assistance and inspiration which they have given me in my work.

*Preface*

I also wish to thank Mr. Andrew Keogh and Mr. Henry A. Gruener for aid in bibliographical matters.

A portion of the expense of printing this book has been borne by the Modern Language Club of Yale University from funds placed at its disposal by the generosity of Mr. George E. Dimock of Elizabeth, New Jersey, a graduate of Yale in the Class of 1874.

YALE UNIVERSITY,                                          F. E. P.
    *July* 31, 1908.

# EDITIONS
## REFERRED TO IN THIS WORK.

For Dekker's *Shoemaker's Holiday*, *Honest Whore*, *Roaring Girl*, and *Old Fortunatus*, the references in this work are to the Mermaid Edition. For all of Dekker's other plays except *Patient Grissil*, the references are to Dekker's *Dramatic Works*, edition of 1873. For *Patient Grissil*, and all of Dekker's non-dramatic works, the references are to Grosart's edition in the Huth Library. The references to Webster are to Dyce's two-column edition of 1857, except that in the *White Devil* I have followed the division of acts and scenes used in the Mermaid Edition. In some cases I have modernized the spelling, but have made no other changes.

# TABLE OF CONTENTS.

## CHAPTER I

# INTRODUCTION.

The collaborated plays of Webster and Dekker are three in number. They consist of the two so-called 'citizen-comedies,' *Westward Ho* and *Northward Ho* —realistic pictures of *bourgeois* life—and a crude, rather uninteresting chronicle-play, called *The Famous History of Sir Thomas Wyatt*. A careful study as to the probable dates of these plays has already been made by Mr. E. E. Stoll. According to this, *Sir Thomas Wyatt* was probably written in 1602, *Westward Ho* in the latter part of 1604 or beginning of 1605, and *Northward Ho* probably in 1606, certainly near that date. [1]

These dates are important, because they mean that at the time of this collaboration Dekker was a mature writer, with a long list of successful plays behind him; Webster was only a beginner. Before 1602 Dekker had written *The Shoemaker's Holiday, Old Fortunatus,* and *Satiro-mastix*, [2] besides a number of plays which have been lost. [3] Between this date and 1605 he had added *Canaan's Calamity, The Wonderful Year, The Bachelor's Banquet, The Magnificent Entertainment given to King James,* and the first part of *The Honest Whore*. [4] Webster, on the other hand, at that date had written nothing which has survived; and there is no record of any play wholly from his hand. Henslowe mentions

---

[1] *John Webster*, by E. E. Stoll, pp. 13—18.
[2] Introduction to Mermaid Ed. of Dekker, pp. XV—XXIV.
[3] *Ibid.*, p. XVI.
[4] *Ibid.*, pp. XXVI—XXX.

Webster as a collaborator in three plays in 1602—all now lost—but the number of other authors mentioned with him would seem to imply that he had but little hand in these works. [1]

Now if we could point out with reasonable definiteness about what were the parts of Webster and Dekker in their collaborated plays, the results would be valuable from several different points of view. In the first place, we should have the scientific satisfaction of settling a matter of fact, and the happy consciousness of giving each writer his due. In the second place, we should gain a glimpse into Webster's intellectual life during his stage of growth. And thirdly, we should throw some light upon the range and limitations of Webster as an author. If Webster wrote the first and third scenes of Act II in *Westward Ho*, or the parts of Captain Jenkins and Hans Van Belch in *Northward Ho*, then he showed an element of pleasant humor and manysidedness which is not indicated anywhere else. If he did not write these and similar scenes in a play where he had a special opportunity to write them, then we shall be strengthened in our old belief that he was an author of great power, but limited range.

The object of this thesis will be to divide the three collaborated plays of Webster and Dekker, and to point out as accurately as possible what seems to be the share of each. In doing this, I shall discuss the two citizen-comedies first, and then take up *Sir Thomas Wyatt* in a chapter by itself.

Some time ago Mr. F. G. Fleay, in his *Biographical Chronicle of the English Drama* (2. 269–271), gave his opinion as to the proper division of acts and scenes. He assigned the last two acts of *Westward Ho* and

---

[1] *John Webster*, by E. E. Stoll, p. 12.

the Doll scenes in *Northward Ho* to Dekker, and all
the rest of the two plays to Webster. For his division
of *Northward Ho* he gave no reasons whatever. His
division of *Westward Ho* was based on two discrepancies in the play. The first of these is that during
Acts I–III the time of the action is referred to as
midsummer, and during Acts IV and V the characters
speak as if the time were late in the fall, and the
weather were frosty. The second discrepancy is that
Mrs. Tenterhook is called Moll in the early part of
the play, and Clare in Act V. Mr. Fleay is right in
saying that these discrepancies exist; but I think he
is mistaken in attaching so much importance to them,
especially when—as Mr. Stoll has already pointed out,
and as we shall show more fully later—the whole
evidence of style and subject-matter is overwhelmingly
against his conclusions. These comedies were probably written in haste, and Dekker was one of the
most careless writers of a careless age. These discrepancies, consequently, could easily be explained
on some other basis than that of different authorship.

In 1905 Mr. E. E. Stoll published a book entitled
*John Webster*, which contains a lengthy and valuable
discussion of these plays. Mr. Stoll makes no attempt
to point out the part of either author definitely, but
contends that Dekker wrote nearly the whole of both
plays, and that Webster's part is both slight and
indeterminate.[1] These conclusions—which flatly contradict those of Mr. Fleay—are based on similarities
of incident and general atmosphere. Though his
arguments are not wholly conclusive, much of the
material which he presents is of unquestionable value,
and will be incorporated into this thesis in its proper
place, with due credit to Mr. Stoll.

[1] *John Webster*, by E. E. Stoll, pp. 62–79.

Such seems to be the state of the question at present. Now in the following pages we will take up a number of different tests which can be applied to these plays, and which will be found to agree surprisingly with one another in their conclusions. The first, which I have called the three-syllable Latin word-test, is, I believe, my own discovery. The second, or parallel-passage test, is old in principle, but has never been worked out in detail for these plays. The other tests have already been taken up by previous students; but I shall try to summarize their work in systematic fashion, together with various additions of my own. Due credit to every one from whom I borrow will be given in the foot-notes.

## CHAPTER II.

# THE THREE-SYLLABLE LATIN WORD-TEST.

If we compare two representative passages, one from Webster and one from Dekker, we become conscious of a difference in their expression which is partly a matter of vocabulary, and partly—in the prose at least—a matter of rhythm. On close analysis, we find that this is largely due to the use of words of Greek or Latin derivation which contain three or more syllables; such words, for example, as *confusion, opinion, politic, immediately, satisfy, remember, misery.* Dekker almost always uses these words sparingly, whereas Webster steadily employs a great number of them. So persistently does Webster adhere to a high percentage of these words, and Dekker to a low percentage, from scene to scene and from play to play, that it becomes a marked characteristic of the style of each, and offers a means for distinguishing the work of one from that of the other.

Now if we turn to the citizen-comedies, we find that five or six scenes in these two plays employ a large number of these words, as Webster does, while all the other scenes have proportionately a much smaller number of these words, as is the case with Dekker. This fact is certainly significant.

In order to put this test on a scientific basis, and free it from the rambling guesswork of vague impressionism, I have tried to reduce the percentage of these three-syllable Greek and Latin words in different scenes to a common standard, so that they could be

mathematically compared and tabulated. This required
a little practical machinery. It is obviously unfair to
compare them by the number of words to a page.
In a scene which is partly in verse and partly in
prose, with broken fragments of lines and wide gaps
between the speeches, it is evident that one page may
contain three times as much solid matter as another.
Therefore the first thing to do, in order to get a fair
basis for comparison, is to reduce the whole scene
in question to solid prose lines; that is, to find how
many lines it would contain if it were printed as one
solid block of prose, without breaks at the ends of
metrical lines, without gaps between speeches, and
without stage-directions. Then the whole number of
three-syllable words (of Greek or Latin derivation)
divided by the number of solid prose lines equals
the ratio of these words to a line. For instance, if
a scene contains 100 solid lines and 22 of the afore-
mentioned words, its word-average would be .220.
If the length of the prose line, which is the standard
of measure, is carefully kept the same, this gives the
fairest and most accurate kind of test. I have taken
as my standard of measure a solid prose line in
Dyce's edition of Webster, and where I have had to
use plays in other editions with longer or shorter
lines, I have carefully reduced them to this standard.[1]
Consequently, when I say in the following tables that
a certain scene contains 100 solid lines, 20 words,
and has a word-average of .200, I mean that it would
contain 100 lines if printed as one solid block of

[1] In computing these tables, I have assumed the following as
equivalent values:

| | | | | | |
|---|---|---|---|---|---|
| One line of normal blank verse | | | | = .85 solid lines in Dyce |
| „ | „ | „ prose, Mermaid Ed. | = 1.07 | „ „ „ „ |
| „ | „ | „ „ Dekker's Works | = 1.03 | „ „ „ „ |
| „ | „ | „ „ Huth Library Ed. | = 1.00 | „ „ „ „ |

prose in Dyce's *Webster*; and that, on an average, in that edition, every five lines would contain one word of three or more syllables which is of Greek or Latin derivation.

Another practical question which had to be settled was just what should be considered as three-syllable Latin words. For example, what should we do with words like *directly* and *instantly*, which consist of a two-syllable Latin stem, and a Germanic suffix. In general, I have included these as wholly Latin, although, rather arbitrarily perhaps, I have cut out the word *presently*, which is so common with all Elizabethans that it interferes with a test, instead of helping it. Whether I have been consistent as to derivation in all minor cases or not, I have tried to be consistent in following the same policy through the different plays of both authors, which would leave the value of the test, as a test, unimpaired.[1]

Now that we have settled the practical machinery of this test, let us look at some of the results. In the following table are given the word-percentages of the different plays of Webster and Dekker taken as whole plays. I have included under Webster the main plot of the *Cure for a Cuckold*. It is uncertain

[1] Owing to the practical difficulty of deciding just what shall be considered Latin words in special cases, a small margin of error should be allowed for in the tables given further on. This margin, however, would never be large enough to affect conclusions materially, and usually would amount to practically nothing. I have observed the following rules throughout this work :

I. Proper names and adjectives denoting nationality, such as *Italian*, are not counted, since they seem to depend more on the subject-matter than on the taste of the author.

II. In three-syllable words of mixed etymology, if the word is two-thirds of Greek or Latin derivation, and this two-thirds includes the main stem of the word, the word is counted as wholly Latin ; otherwise it is not counted.

whether Webster wrote the whole of the main plot
or not; but he probably wrote most of it,[1] and almost
certainly did not write the underplot. I have also
included *Patient Grissil* under Dekker, although it is
a collaborated play, since Dekker probably wrote most
of it.[2] It is worth while, however, to remember that
there are scenes in these two plays which were
probably not written by either Dekker or Webster.

| *Average.* | *Webster's Plays.* |
|---|---|
| .349 | Duchess of Malfi. |
| .342 | White Devil. |
| .328 | Appius and Virginia. |
| .311 | Devil's Law Case. |
| .296 | Cure for a Cuckold [main plot]. |

| | *Dekker's Plays.* |
|---|---|
| .252 | Whore of Babylon. |
| .247 | Old Fortunatus. |
| .225 | The Devil is in It. |
| .213 | Satiro-mastix. |
| .193 | Patient Grissil [collaborated]. |
| .174 | Honest Whore, Part I [slightly collaborated]. |
| .172 | Wonder of a Kingdom. |
| .153 | Honest Whore, Part II. |
| .147 | Match Me in London. |
| .116 | Shoemaker's Holiday. |

A glance at the above table shows that the general
word-percentage of Dekker's plays is far below that
of Webster's, irrespective of subject-matter or anything
else. A gap of 40 points lies between the lowest
play of Webster (even if he wrote it all) and the
highest play of Dekker. But this is not all. We are
discussing these plays in order to pass a judgment
on the authorship of the citizen-comedies, and hence

[1] *John Webster*, by E. E. Stoll, pp. 34–43.
[2] Dekker's *Non-Dramatic Works*, Huth Library, Vol. V, p. 110.

are chiefly interested in those plays of Dekker which are closest to the citizen-comedies in matter and spirit. Now it is obvious that the three plays which stand highest on Dekker's list are the very three which are most remote from the citizen-comedies in these respects. *The Whore of Babylon,* [1] *Old Fortunatus,* and *The Devil is in It* are all abstract, romantic, semi-allegorical in character, and separated by a wide gap from the simple, middle-class realism of Dekker's other plays, and of *Northward* and *Westward Ho.* For a fair comparison, then, of Webster and Dekker, as Dekker would be in a *bourgeois* comedy, we should begin Dekker's list with *Satiro-mastix,* and the gap between that and *A Cure for a Cuckold* is 83 points.

Now, with these preceding tables in mind, let us look at the separate scenes in the two citizen-comedies.

### Westward Ho.

| Act and Scene. | Solid lines. | Words. | Average to line. |
|---|---|---|---|
| I. 1 | 251 | 77 | .307 |
| 2 | 130 | 28 | .215 |
| II. 1 | 242 | 41 | .169 |
| 2 | 270 | 40 | .148 |
| 3 | 129 | 20 | .155 |
| III. 1 | 52 | 13 | .250 |
| 2 | 112 | 26 | .234 |
| 3 | 132 | 44 | .333 |
| 4 | 65 | 14 | .215 |
| IV. 1 | 242 | 41 | .169 |
| 2 | 202 | 30 | .149 |
| V. 1 | 270 | 54 | .200 |
| 2 | 8 | 0 | |
| 3 | 84 | 10 | .119 |
| 4 | 332 | 56 | .169 |

[1] It should be remembered, also, that some critics consider the authorship of *The Whore of Babylon* uncertain.

*Northward Ho.*

| Act and Scene. | Solid lines. | Words. | Average to line. |
| --- | --- | --- | --- |
| I. 1 | 193 | 58 | .301 |
| 2 | 108 | 20 | .185 |
| 3 | 181 | 18 | .100 |
| II. 1 | 284 | 22 | .078 |
| 2 | 201 | 63 | .313 |
| III. 1 | 127 | 35 | .276 |
| 2 | 142 | 26 | .183 |
| IV. 1 | 287 | 64 | .223 |
| 2 | 39 | 7 | .179 |
| 3 | 178 | 19 | .107 |
| V. A[1] | 384 | 131 | .341 |
| B | 162 | 24 | .148 |

It will be noticed at once that I. 1 and III. 3 in *Westward Ho*, and I. 1, II. 2, and V. A in *Northward Ho*, are above .300; that only two scenes, one of them very short—III. 1 in *Westward Ho* and III. 1 in *Northward Ho*—lie in that wide gap between .300 and .234; and that all the other scenes are below .234, all but two of them below 216. The very width of this great empty gap seems in itself to be a silent witness of a dividing line. Then it will be remembered that the lowest of Webster's plays has an average of just barely below .300, and that the highest of Dekker's realistic comedies stops at .213.

Now, from a lawyer's point of view, this would be a good place to halt. But we are not trying to build up a case, but to find the truth, whether that truth agrees with our theories or not; hence a further search is necessary. Hitherto we have been comparing separate scenes in *Northward Ho* and *Westward*

[1] Act V is all one scene. I have divided it for very obvious reasons into Parts A and B. B begins at the stage-direction, *Enter Philip, Leverpool, and Chartley.*

*Ho* with whole plays. This obviously is not fair. To be consistent and sure of our ground, we must make certain that the separate scenes in the uncollaborated plays do not vary like the separate scenes in the collaborated plays, whatever their final average. The average of *Westward Ho* as a complete play is only .190; and if we had followed that, we should have given the whole play to Dekker. This means that we need a tabulated examination of all the plays by Webster and Dekker, scene by scene. If they will stand examination in this way, we shall know that we are building upon bed-rock. As a matter of fact, we shall find that there are a few scenes in Webster which are quite low, and a few scenes in Dekker which are quite high; but that these exceptions in both cases are exceedingly rare, and that nearly all the high scenes of Dekker are from *The Whore of Babylon, Old Fortunatus,* and *The Devil is in It,* the very three plays which, as we have already observed, are least in point in discussing realistic middle-class comedy.

PLAYS OF WEBSTER.

*Duchess of Malfi.*

| Act and Scene. | Solid lines. | Words. | Average. |
|---|---|---|---|
| I. 1 | 424 | 166 | .391 |
| II. 1 | 161 | 55 | .342 |
| 2 | 70 | 14 | .200 |
| 3 | 67 | 25 | .373 |
| 4 | 71 | 28 | .394 |
| 5 | 67 | 23 | .343 |
| III. 1 | 78 | 34 | .436 |
| 2 | 275 | 91 | .331 |
| 3 | 61 | 27 | .443 |
| 4 | 23 | 11 | .478 |
| 5 | 117 | 33 | .282 |

| Act and Scene. | Solid lines. | Words. | Average. |
|---|---|---|---|
| IV. 1 | 116 | 47 | .405 |
| 2 | 296 | 98 | .331 |
| V. 1 | 64 | 24 | .375 |
| 2 | 279 | 97 | .347 |
| 3 | 48 | 16 | .333 |
| 4 | 65 | 20 | .308 |
| 5 | 97 | 21 | .216 |

*White Devil.*

| | | | |
|---|---|---|---|
| I. 1 | 53 | 22 | .415 |
| 2 | 313 | 106 | .339 |
| II. 1 | 268 | 82 | .306 |
| 2 | 63 | 12 | .190 |
| 3 | 48 | 15 | .312 |
| 4 | 63 | 29 | .460 |
| III. 1 | 383 | 165 | .430 |
| 2 | 112 | 40 | .357 |
| IV. 1 | 203 | 69 | .339 |
| 2 | 119 | 50 | .420 |
| V. 1 | 210 | 63 | .300 |
| 2 | 68 | 14 | .206 |
| 3 | 215 | 70 | .326 |
| 4 | 125 | 30 | .240 |
| 5 | 13 | 6 | .461 |
| 6 | 256 | 87 | .340 |

*Appius and Virginia.*

| | | | |
|---|---|---|---|
| I. 1 | 115 | 43 | .374 |
| 2 | 38 | 12 | .316 |
| 3 | 172 | 49 | .285 |
| II. 1 | 72 | 34 | .472 |
| 2 | 179 | 76 | .424 |
| 3 | 171 | 51 | .298 |
| III. 1 | 102 | 27 | .265 |
| 2 | 305 | 89 | .292 |

| Act and Scene. | Solid lines. | Words. | Average. |
|---|---|---|---|
| 3 | 23 | 10 | .435 |
| 4 | 69 | 8 | .116 |
| IV. 1 | 258 | 92 | .356 |
| 2 | 153 | 48 | .314 |
| V. 1 | 40 | 16 | .400 |
| 2 | 95 | 30 | .316 |
| 3 | 151 | 53 | .351 |

*Devil's Law Case.*

| | | | |
|---|---|---|---|
| I. 1 | 166 | 49 | .295 |
| 2 | 224 | 64 | .286 |
| II. 1 | 270 | 86 | .318 |
| 2 | 39 | 13 | .333 |
| 3 | 130 | 40 | .307 |
| 4 | 37 | 12 | .324 |
| III. 1 | 24 | 5 | .208 |
| 2 | 133 | 43 | .323 |
| 3 | 326 | 124 | .380 |
| IV. 1 | 93 | 30 | .323 |
| 2 | 508 | 154 | .303 |
| V. 1 | 33 | 5 | .151 |
| 2 | 34 | 9 | .265 |
| 3 | 26 | 8 | .308 |
| 4 | 142 | 38 | .267 |
| 5 | 20 | 5 | .250 |
| 6 | 72 | 23 | .319 |

*Cure for a Cuckold.*

(Underplot scenes, and parts of scenes, are bracketed.)

| | | | |
|---|---|---|---|
| I. 1 | 149 | 47 | .318 |
| 2 | 163 | 48 | .294 |
| II. 1 | 42 | 10 | .238 |
| 2 | 85 | 30 | .353 |
| [3] | [156] | [15] | [.096] |
| 4 | 133 | 27 | .203 |

| Act and Scene. | Solid lines. | Words. | Average. |
|---|---|---|---|
| III. 1 | 122 | 42 | .344 |
| [2] | [100] | [9] | [.090] |
| 3 | 89 | 25 | .281 |
| IV. [1] | [213] | [41] | [.193] |
| 2 | 170 | 53 | .313 |
| [3] | [124] | [24] | [.194] |
| V. 1 | 230 | 69 | .300 |
| 2, A. | 71 | 20 | .282 |
| [2, B][1] | [52] | [10] | [.192] |

## DEKKER'S PLAYS.

### A.—Romantic and allegorical plays.

#### *Whore of Babylon.*

| Scenes and pages.[2] | Solid lines. | Words. | Average. |
|---|---|---|---|
| I. (192–201) | 211 | 62 | .293 |
| II. (201–211) | 241 | 66 | .274 |
| III. (211–220) | 246 | 63 | .256 |
| IV. (220–226) | 154 | 28 | .182 |
| V. (227–235) | 225 | 73 | .320 |
| VI. (235–241) | 137 | 43 | .314 |
| VII. (241–246) | 124 | 27 | .218 |
| VIII. (246–252) | 150 | 20 | .133 |
| IX. (253–259) | 151 | 53 | .329[3] |
| X. (259–269) | 259 | 53 | .205 |
| XI. (269–271) | 54 | 13 | .241 |
| XII. (271–275) | 101 | 20 | .198 |
| XIII. (275–278) | 42 | 10 | .238 |

[1] Scene divided at, *Enter Compass, Raymond*, etc.
[2] Pages cited are those in Dekker's *Dramatic Works*, ed. 1873.
[3] Contains a proclamation which has 18 lines and 15 words. Without the proclamation, it averages below .270

## Old Fortunatus.

| Act and Scene. | Solid lines. | Words. | Average. |
|---|---|---|---|
| I. 1 | 295 | 86 | .292 |
| 2 | 200 | 30 | .150 |
| 3 | 83 | 23 | .277 |
| II. 1 | 105 | 24 | .229 |
| 2 | 375 | 104 | .277 |
| III. 1 | 304 | 86 | .283 |
| 2 | 135 | 32 | .237 |
| IV. 1 | 199 | 35 | .176 |
| 2 | 122 | 31 | .254 |
| V. 1 | 166 | 36 | .217 |
| 2 | 304 | 86 | .283 |

## The Devil is in It.

| Scenes and pages. | Solid lines. | Words. | Average. |
|---|---|---|---|
| I. (265–271) | 110 | 22 | .200 |
| II. (271–280) | 198 | 38 | .192 |
| III. (280–287) | 164 | 56 | .341[1] |
| IV. (287–295) | 183 | 19 | .104 |
| V. (295–303) | 166 | 27 | .163 |
| VI. (303–307) | 71 | 19 | .268 |
| VII. (307–308) | 46 | 10 | .218 |
| VIII. (308–314) | 126 | 27 | .214 |
| IX. (314–322) | 150 | 30 | .200 |
| X. (322–325) | 71 | 17 | .239 |
| XI. (325–330) | 117 | 25 | .214 |
| XII. (330–331) | 31 | 4 | .129 |
| XIII. (331–334) | 52 | 15 | .288 |
| XIV. (334–348) | 294 | 71 | .242 |
| XV. (348–359) | 218 | 58 | .266 |

[1] Scene at monastery, full of semi-technical religious terms.

B.—Realistic comedies like the citizen-comedies.

### *Satiro-mastix.*

| Scenes and pages. | Solid lines. | Words. | Average. |
|---|---|---|---|
| I. (185–191) | 150 | 20 | .133 |
| II. (191–203) | 353 | 68 | .193 |
| III. (203–211) | 190 | 29 | .153 |
| IV. (211–213) | 60 | 14 | .233 |
| V. (213–222) | 249 | 41 | .165 |
| VI. (222–225) | 66 | 11 | .167 |
| VII. (225–232) | 188 | 41 | .218 |
| VIII. (232–238) | 166 | 41 | .247 |
| IX. (238–246) | 248 | 64 | .258 |
| X. (246–252) | 151 | 29 | .192 |
| XI. (252–264) | 326 | 92 | .282 |

### *Patient Grissil* [collaborated].

| Act and Scene. | Solid lines. | Words. | Average. |
|---|---|---|---|
| I. 1 | 66 | 15 | .227 |
| 2 | 302 | 43 | .142 |
| II. 1 | 302 | 81 | .268 |
| 2 | 144 | 27 | .187 |
| III. 1 | 149 | 42 | .282 |
| 2 | 260 | 71 | .273 |
| IV. 1 | 198 | 34 | .172 |
| 2 | 191 | 27 | .141 |
| 3 | 272 | 25 | .092 |
| V. 1 | 90 | 18 | .200 |
| 2 | 280 | 54 | .193 |

### *Honest Whore, Part I.*

| I. 1 | 125 | 30 | .240 |
|---|---|---|---|
| 2 | 126 | 15 | .119 |
| 3 | 84 | 18 | .215 |

| Act and Scene. | Solid lines. | Words. | Average. |
|---|---|---|---|
| 4 | 55 | 18 | .327[1] |
| 5 | 181 | 32 | .177 |
| II. 1 | 376 | 72 | .192 |
| III. 1 | 216 | 34 | .157 |
| 2 | 76 | 18 | .237 |
| 3 | 102 | 28 | .274 |
| IV. 1 | 162 | 27 | .167 |
| 2 | 44 | 5 | .114 |
| 3 | 142 | 15 | .106 |
| 4 | 99 | 22 | .222 |
| V. 1 | 98 | 18 | .184 |
| 2 | 419 | 49 | .117 |

### *Wonder of a Kingdom.*

| Act and Scene. | Solid lines. | Words. | Average. |
|---|---|---|---|
| I. 1 | 82 | 11 | .134 |
| 2 | 77 | 10 | .130 |
| 3 | 75 | 11 | .147 |
| 4 | 134 | 29 | .217 |
| II. 1 | 112 | 15 | .134 |
| 2 | 145 | 29 | .200 |
| III. 1 | 190 | 35 | .184 |
| 2 | 75 | 15 | .200 |
| 3 | 43 | 5 | .117 |
| IV. 1 | 49 | 11 | .224 |
| 2 | 155 | 41 | .264 |
| 3 | 53 | 7 | .132 |
| 4 | 49 | 5 | .102 |
| V. 1 | 47 | 7 | .149 |
| 2 | 123 | 12 | .098 |

[1] Possibly the work of Middleton, who had some slight share in this play. It is near that part of the play in which Mr. Bullen thinks that he sees traces of Middleton's hand.

*Honest Whore, Part II.*

| Act and Scene. | Solid lines. | Words. | Average. |
|---|---|---|---|
| I. 1 | 150 | 15 | .100 |
| 2 | 184 | 21 | .114 |
| 3 | 102 | 18 | .176 |
| II. 1 | 220 | 24 | .109 |
| 2 | 100 | 5 | .050 |
| III. 1 | 187 | 20 | .107 |
| 2 | 124 | 9 | .073 |
| 3 | 92 | 6 | .065 |
| IV. 1 | 322 | 55 | .171 |
| 2 | 95 | 11 | .116 |
| 3 | 131 | 28 | .214 |
| V. 1 | 23 | 3 | .130 |
| 2 | 408 | 75 | .184 |

*Match Me in London.*

| Pages. | | | |
|---|---|---|---|
| I. 1 (135–142) | 135 | 11 | .081 |
| 2 (142–149) | 160 | 19 | .119 |
| II. 1 (150–158) | 187 | 28 | .149 |
| 2 (158–162) | 92 | 11 | .120 |
| 3 (162–168) | 94 | 11 | .117 |
| III. 1 (168–176) | 156 | 24 | .154 |
| 2 (176–184) | 168 | 29 | .173 |
| 3 (184–188) | 90 | 7 | .078 |
| IV. 1 (188–194) | 130 | 19 | .146 |
| 2 (194–197) | 66 | 13 | .197 |
| 3 (197–201) | 86 | 15 | .198 |
| 4 (202–206) | 77 | 18 | .234 |
| V. 1 (206–212) | 115 | 15 | .130 |
| 2 (212–216) | 85 | 21 | .247 |

*Shoemaker's Holiday.*

| | | | |
|---|---|---|---|
| I. 1 | 211 | 43 | .204 |
| II. 1 | 62 | 12 | .193 |

| Act and Scene. | Solid lines. | Words. | Average. |
|---|---|---|---|
| 2 | 20 | 2 | .100 |
| 3 | 105 | 5 | .048 |
| 4 | 14 | 2 | .143 |
| 5 | 55 | 2 | .036 |
| III. 1 | 123 | 11 | .089 |
| 2 | 46 | 9 | .196 |
| 3 | 88 | 12 | .136 |
| 4 | 141 | 13 | .092 |
| 5 | 88 | 9 | .102 |
| IV. 1 | 105 | 11 | .105 |
| 2 | 42 | 3 | .071 |
| 3 | 64 | 5 | .078 |
| 4 | 40 | 6 | .150 |
| 5 | 134 | 8 | .060 |
| V. 1 | 55 | 5 | .090 |
| 2 | 189 | 19 | .101 |
| 3 | 13 | 5 | .384 [1] |
| 4 | 70 | 8 | .114 |
| 5 | 167 | 22 | .132 |

The above results would seem to be striking enough in themselves; but they will become more so under a little examination. In the first place, we must lay it down as a law that the value of the word-test varies with the length of the scene. In both Dekker and Webster the word-average frequently does not move along a plane, but varies up and down with a kind of wave-motion, which adjusts itself to a proper sea-level within the length of a reasonably long scene. There are many short passages in Dekker which, taken by themselves, would have a word-average of over .300, when the whole scene from which they are taken is below .200. In the same way, very low short

[1] Too short to count; see discussion later.

passages could be culled from scenes in Webster, which, as scenes, are high. Roughly speaking, we may say that the word-test is decidedly unreliable in a scene of fewer than thirty lines, and much stronger in one of a hundred lines than in one of sixty. In *Westward Ho* and *Northward Ho* the scenes are long, twenty-two of them, out of a total of twenty-six,[1] being well above one hundred lines; hence the test here is quite reliable.

Now if we glance at the preceding tables, we find that most of Webster's lowest scenes and some of Dekker's highest scenes are very short; and that the average of the former would be very much raised, that of the latter much lowered, by including them with adjacent scenes. For instance, V. 3 of *The Shoe-maker's Holiday* has an average of .384; but it contains only 13 solid lines, and if it were included in either one of the adjacent scenes, the whole would have an average far below .200.

Again, if we read over some of Dekker's high-average scenes in the semi-allegorical plays, we find that there are forces in them which exert an abnormal influence on the vocabulary. For instance, *The Whore of Babylon* is the story of a religious war; and in the councils of the Catholic leaders such words as *heresy, excommunicate, absolution,* etc., are inevitably drawn upon in great numbers. Likewise, Scene III of *The Devil is in It* is at a monastery; and its remarkable average of .341 is largely due to this inevitable element in the speech of churchmen. Even then, this one scene in *The Devil is in It*, and three scenes in *The Whore of Babylon*, are the only ones in

---

[1] Not counting the chamberlain-scene, V. 2, which is a mere fragment of eight lines.

these plays which rise above .300; and one of these three scenes in *The Whore of Babylon* would drop below .270 if we excluded a short and very elaborate proclamation, which is not at all a fair representative of dramatic dialogue. So Dekker under abnormal conditions maintains a lower level than Webster does under normal ones; and the moment that Dekker's surroundings become normal, a magic circle seems to hold even his highest scenes well below .300.

There are two short scenes which deserve special consideration. The first is I. 4 in *Part I* of *The Honest Whore*. This is not under any abnormal influence, but a simple fragment of commonplace life; yet its word-average is .327. It is a short scene (55 lines); but its size, though small enough to diminish the value of the word-test, is not small enough to render it worthless. We know that Middleton had some part in this play, and the most satisfactory theory would be that he wrote the scene in question. Even if he did not, it would simply be the exception which proves the rule, since it is the only scene of *bourgeois* life in all Dekker's plays which has an average above .300.

The other scene which needs discussion is *Appius and Virginia* III. 4. This is by far the lowest scene in Webster, having an average of only .116; and, although it is not a long scene (69 lines), it is too long to be lightly thrown aside. Now there are several peculiar things about this scene. In the first place, it is wholly in prose, except for one scrap of doggerel rime. Now Webster does not usually have whole scenes in prose, nor is he fond of doggerel rime. Secondly, the scene does not advance the action at all;[1]

[1] To be sure, Corbulo says that Numitorius has sent a messenger to Virginius; but the audience have already seen the messenger sent at the end of III. 2.

it could be left out, and no one would know the
difference.   Thirdly, there is nothing in the scene,
from beginning to end, which sounds like the Webster we know.  In short, this scene has all the earmarks
of an interpolation; and, in general character, it is
just such a scene as might be put in to amuse the
groundlings.

The general results of this detailed examination of
Dekker's and Webster's plays may be summed up in
the following tables.   Table I includes all scenes,
irrespective of conditions.   Table II omits the
two doubtful scenes discussed above, omits *The
Whore of Babylon, Old Fortunatus*, and *The Devil is in It*
altogether, and considers every scene of less than
60 lines as part of the shortest adjacent scene.   The
first table compares Webster and Dekker in general.
The second table compares Webster with Dekker as
he appears in the *bourgeois* comedies under discussion.

## Table I.

|                          | *Webster*       | *Dekker*        |
|--------------------------|-----------------|-----------------|
| Total number of scenes   | 74              | 140             |
| Scenes above .299        | 51 or 68.9%     | 6 or 4.3%       |
| Scenes .299–.275         | 9 or 12.2%      | 9 or 6.1%       |
| Scenes .274–.225         | 6 or 8.1%       | 23 or 16.4%     |
| Scenes .225–.200         | 5 or 6.8%       | 17 or 12.1%     |
| Scenes below .200        | 3 or 4.1%       | 85 or 60.7%     |

## Table II.

|                          | *Webster*       | *Dekker*        |
|--------------------------|-----------------|-----------------|
| Total number of scenes   | 60              | 88              |
| Scenes above .299        | 41 or 68.3%     | none            |
| Scenes .299–.275         | 10 or 16.7%     | 2 or 2.3%       |
| Scenes .274–.225         | 5 or 8.3%       | 12 or 13.6%     |
| Scenes .224–.200         | 4 or 6.7%       | 9 or 10.2%      |
| Scenes below .200        | none            | 65 or 73.9%     |

Now, even if we should take the most unfavorable attitude possible toward our theory, and base our calculations on Table I instead of Table II, we should still, according to the mathematical theory of chances, have the following results: (a) When a scene has a word-average of .300 or over, the chances are 68.9 to 4.3, or 16 to 1, that Webster, and not Dekker, wrote it; (b) when a scene is below .200, the chances are 60.7 to 4.1, or 15 to 1, that Dekker, and not Webster, wrote it. This disposes at once of 19 scenes out of 26. Again, since only 11 per cent. of Webster's scenes (only 7 per cent. in Table II) are below .225, there is but little chance that Webster had very much part in any of the 5 scenes between .200 and .225. These were probably either written wholly by Dekker, or else written largely by him, with some little help from Webster. Two scenes are now left unassigned. For III. 1 of *Westward Ho* the word-test must be pronounced almost worthless. Not only is its brief length a drawback, but, much more important, its average of .250 is the most indeterminate number possible. In this scene we must depend on other tests. III. 1 of *Northward Ho* will perhaps be best understood if we analyze the word-averages of the different characters. They are as follows:

### *Northward Ho* III. 1.

|  | Solid lines. | Words. | Average. |
|---|---|---|---|
| Doll . . . . . . | 67 | 14 | .209 |
| Philip . . . . . | 31 | 15 | .484 |
| Bellamont . . . | 22 | 6 | .273 |
| Minor characters . | 7 | 0 | .000 |
| Totals | 127 | 35 | .276 |

I do not think the above *proves* that Webster wrote the parts of Philip and Bellamont[1], because when a scene is slashed into such small fragments, the word-test loses much of its value; but nevertheless the above figures are certainly suspicious.

One word more. Since the citizen-plays are wholly in prose, and since we wish to be sure of our ground, it may be worth while to glance in passing at Dekker's non-dramatic prose. Now there is a certain minor part of Dekker's prose, of which *The Gull's Hornbook* is the best example, which, instead of having a low average, has one about as high as that of Webster's plays. However, this is easily explained. *The Gull's Hornbook* is absolutely undramatic throughout, without dialogue, and written wholly in a mock-heroic vein. Its burlesque grandiloquence explains its high average. But the great mass of Dekker's prose, and especially that part of it which approaches nearest to comedy, has the same low word-average as his plays. The best example of this is *The Bachelor's Banquet*, which is closer to comedy in general, and far closer to *Westward Ho* in particular, than any other of his non-dramatic works. The following table shows the word-test in *The Bachelor's Banquet*:

| Chapter. | Solid lines. | Words. | Average. |
|---|---|---|---|
| I | 367 | 81 | .220 |
| II | 161 | 34 | .211 |
| III | 483 | 64 | .132 |
| IV | 196 | 25 | .128 |
| V | 334 | 47 | .140 |
| VI | 241 | 36 | .149 |

[1] Webster could not have written every word of their speeches, as is shown by the parallel-passage test; but he may have written most of them.

| Chapter. | Solid lines. | Words. | Average. |
|---|---|---|---|
| VII | 228 | 48 | .210 |
| VIII | 182 | 20 | .110 |
| IX | 222 | 31 | .140 |
| X | 99 | 24 | .242 |
| XI | 263 | 62 | .236 |
| XII | 75 | 20 | .266 |
| XIII | 115 | 34 | .296 |
| XIV | 140 | 51 | .364 |
| XV | 219 | 37 | .169 |
| Totals 3325 | | 614 | .185 |

Not only is the general average in this book low, but the lowest chapters are the most dramatic, contain the most dialogue and the most character-photography. The higher chapters are those in which this fades away into a burlesque monologue; and the highest chapter in the book (Chapter XIV, average .364) is one of the few chapters in the whole work which do not contain a single word of dialogue, but resembles rather the mock-heroic tone of *The Gull's Hornbook*.

To conclude, then, the further we examine the works of Webster and Dekker, the more evidence we find that the former almost invariably[1] has a high word-average, and that the latter, as a playwright at least, consistently has a very low one. Consequently, when we find five or six scenes in the citizen-comedies

---

[1] The following table shows the word-averages of the few short poems which Webster has left us:

| | | | |
|---|---|---|---|
| Monumental Column | 279 | 88 | .315 |
| To Munday  .  .  . | 10 | 5 | |
| Ode  .  .  .  .  .  . | 16 | 4 | |
| To Heywood  .  .  . | 19 | 6 | |
| To Cockeran  .  .  . | 7 | 0 | |
| Totals 331 | | 103 | .311 |

with Webster's high average, nineteen or twenty with Dekker's low average, and a wide, almost empty gap between, we are justified in assuming that Webster wrote—not all perhaps—but certainly the larger part of the former scenes; and that Dekker wrote all or nearly all of the latter. We might expect to find some casual trace of Dekker's revising touches in the higher scenes, or of Webster's in the lower; but we certainly should not expect that either of these writers would have any considerable part in such scenes.

The word-test, then, would seem to indicate the following division of scenes:

*Webster's Part.*

*Westward Ho*, I. 1 and III. 3.

*Northward Ho*, I. 1; II. 2; V. A.

*Dekker's Part.*

*Westward Ho*, I. 2; II.; III. 2; III. 4; IV; V.

*Northward Ho*, I. 2; I. 3; II. 1; III. 2; IV; V. B.

*Uncertain.*

*Westward Ho*, III. 1.

*Northward Ho*, III. 1.

It will be noticed that this test, while not going quite so far as Mr. Stoll, in the main agrees with him in giving by far the larger part of the two plays to Dekker.

Of course we realize that this test, like any test, is not absolutely infallible. But when we consider that the plays of Dekker which we have discussed range through every walk of life and every phase of human emotion, from the king's palace in *Match Me in London* to the home of the day laborer in the *Shoemaker's Holiday*, from the pure presence of Jane to the reeking atmosphere of the brothel, from the tragedy of Hippolito's grief and the Duke's dignified

anger to the vulgar mirth of prentices and bawds,
and that through all this he steadily keeps a low
word-average, while Webster has a high one, we
must admit that this test has a decided value.[1]   And
if we can support this test by other evidence agreeing
with it, we may hope, in part of the scenes at least,
to arrive at what a court would call reasonable proof.
A considerable amount of such supporting evidence
will be found in the following chapters.

[1] One interesting proof of the value of this test is found by
tracing the word-average of a single character from scene to
scene. If a single character is the work of one author, we
should certainly expect such a character to be reasonably consistent in vocabulary. On the contrary, the language of Birdlime
and Justiniano in *Westward Ho*, and of Bellamont and Mayberry
in *Northward Ho*, varies remarkably.

|  | Birdlime |  |  |
|---|---|---|---|
| *Westward Ho.* | Solid lines. | Words. | Average. |
| I. 1 | 104 | 36 | .346 |
| II. 2 | 156 | 18 | .116 |
| II. 3 | 5 | 1 | (too short) |
| IV. 1 | 99 | 17 | .172 |
| V. 3 | 28 | 3 | .107 (short) |
| V. 4 | 23 | 1 | .043 (short) |
|  | Justiniano. |  |  |
| I. 1 | 92 | 23 | .250 |
| II. 1 | 152 | 24 | .158 |
| II. 3 | 54 | 12 | .222 |
| III. 3 | 106 | 38 | .358 |
| IV. 1 | 20 | 6 | .300 (too short) |
| IV. 2 | 103 | 13 | .126 |
| V. 4 | 140 | 27 | .193 |
|  | Bellamont. |  |  |
| *Northward Ho.* |  |  |  |
| I. 1 | 52 | 18 | .346 |
| I. 3 | 45 | 3 | .067 |
| II. 2 | 46 | 23 | .500 |
| III. 1 | 22 | 6 | .273 (short) |
| IV. 1 | 108 | 31 | .287 |
| IV. 3 | 62 | 2 | .032 |
| V. A | 176 | 72 | .409 |
| V. B | 42 | 6 | .143 |

Bellamont's rather high average in IV. 1 may possibly be due merely to his affected style, since he is talking here in poetry ; it is probably a burlesque on Chapman's grandiloquence. But the radical extremes in the other scenes cannot be explained.

Mayberry.

| *Northward Ho.* | Solid lines. | Words. | Average. |
|---|---|---|---|
| I. 1 | 54 | 7 | .130 |
| I. 3 | 60 | 5 | .083 |
| II. 2 | 57 | 20 | .351 |
| IV. 1 | 62 | 9 | .145 |
| IV. 3 | 15 | 1 | (too short) |
| V. A | 37 | 8 | .216 (short) |
| V. B | 51 | 5 | .098 |

In I. 1 Mayberry's low average in a high-average scene seems rather suspicious, especially as his total part is nearly 60 lines in length. His change of heart in II. 2 is certainly peculiar.

## CHAPTER III.

# THE PARALLEL-PASSAGE TEST.
## *WESTWARD HO.*

The value of parallel passages as a test of author-ship has been almost universally recognized. Now if this is true of authors in general, it certainly is true of Dekker and Webster; for each of these men has the habit of repeating his own phrases from play to play, until it becomes a positive mannerism. Mr. Stoll has already published a long list of almost *verbatim* parallels from the various plays of Webster,[1] and a still longer list of similar parallels between his own plays might easily be gathered from the works of Dekker. On the other hand, while each of these writers constantly repeats himself, neither shows any tendency in later plays to repeat the phraseology of the other. Five or six parallelisms[2] may be pointed

---

[1] *John Webster*, pp. 80—82.

[2] Dyce has the following:

*White Devil*, p. 21:

They are first
Sweetmeats which rot the eater.

*Whore of Babylon*, 1607, Sig. I. 2:

Good words,
Sweetmeats which rot the eater.

*Duchess of Malfi* III. 2:

Our weak safety
Runs upon enginous wheels.

*Whore of Babylon*, 1607, Sig. C. 2:

For that one act gives, like an enginous wheel,
Motion to all.

I have been unable to find more than two or three other parallels in carefully reading all the works of both authors.

out in the whole range of their writing, and that is all. Possibly a critic would have the right to contend in the same way that one or two of the parallel passages following might be likewise due to chance or imitation ; but such would constitute a mere drop in the bucket. No man in general forms the habit of using his friends' little turns of phrase ; thus Webster and Dekker habitually repeat themselves, but neither the other. Consequently, when we find from three to twelve parallel passages in a single scene from one author, we have every right to consider it as the strongest kind of evidence for his authorship. Like all other evidence, it is cumulative, and the greater the number of passages, the stronger is the proof.

One word of explanation should be given in regard to the following passages. Besides the parallels which are of unquestionable value, the student often finds a number which present a rather shadowy likeness ; and he frequently hesitates as to whether they are worth including or not. Since opinions often differ as to the exact value of passages, and since it is obviously better to include several almost worthless ones than to lose one good one, I have retained a number which are, I think, of some value, but far from convincing. The reader is requested to consider all the evidence at its real worth, and not be prejudiced too much by a single passage which is either very strong or very weak. For the sake of convenience, I have, in a number of cases, recorded my own opinion at the end of the passage. A question-mark in brackets at the end of a passage means that I do not consider the passage very strong, although I have thought it worth including. A single asterisk in brackets means that the passages owe some of their parallelism to a proverbial expression or literary tradition, but that nevertheless the parallelism seems valuable as proof.

There is another consideration which is very important in estimating the shares of Webster and Dekker in any particular scene. Dekker's extant works, including practically all of nine plays, large parts of several others, and four or five volumes of non-dramatic writing, form a total about four times as bulky as all that Webster has left us. Consequently, when Dekker uses a particular phrase in *Westward Ho*, he has about four times as many chances as Webster has of using it again elsewhere. Again, many of Dekker's other plays are more or less similar in spirit to *Westward Ho*; therefore phrases which he had used before in earlier similar plays would naturally bubble up in this play; and phrases which had been used in this play would, by the law of association of ideas, rise spontaneously in the similar scenes of later plays. Most of Webster's other works, on the contrary, are dignified, heavy tragedy, in verse instead of prose; and consequently the phrases which he had used in an early *bourgeois* comedy would not be nearly so apt to reappear. These two facts should always be borne in mind; for we shall find several scenes with a high word-average in which the parallel passages from the two poets seem at first sight of about equal value. But when we consider these two facts, we realize that Webster must have had by far the larger share, and that Dekker probably simply retouched the scene.

The following are the parallel passages which I have collected for *Westward Ho*.

Westward Ho.

Act I, Scene 1.

(251 solid lines; word-average, 307.)

Passages from Webster.

(a) *Westward Ho* I. 1: Stay, tailor, this is the house.

*Devil's Law Case* III. 2: But stay, I lose myself, this is the house.

(b) *Westward Ho* I. 1: But your lady or justice-o'-the-peace madam carries high wit from the city [i. e. from the city dames, ladies learn from *bourgeoises*], namely, to receive all and pay all, to awe their husbands, to check their husbands, to control their husbands,

*Devil's Law Case* I. 1: Leonora [a merchant's wife.] Indeed, the Exchange bell makes us dine so late, | I think the ladies of the court from us | Learn to lie so long abed.

*Devil's Law Case* III. 1: Why, they use their lords as if they were their wards, | And, as your Dutch women in the Low Countries | Take all and pay all, and do keep their husbands | So silly all their lives of their own estate.

nay, they have the trick on't to be sick for a new gown.

*Duchess of Malfi* III. 2. You had the trick in audit time to be sick.

Also for the triple formation of the sentence in 'to awe their husbands, to check their husbands, to control their husbands,' compare

*White Devil* III. 1: There are not Jews enough, priests enough, nor gentlemen enough.

(c) *Westward Ho* I. 1: My good old lord and master, that hath been a tilter this twenty year, hath sent it. [*]

*White Devil* II. 4: For none are judges at tilting but those who have been old tilters.

*White Devil* I. 2: Camillo—a lousy slave, that within this twenty years rode with the black guard.

(d) *Westward Ho* I. 1: O the entertainment my lord will make you, — sweet wines, lusty diet, perfumed linen, soft beds.

*White Devil* I. 2. Thou shalt lie in a bed stuffed with turtles' feathers; swoon in perfumed linen.

(e) *Westward Ho* I. 1: No German clock, nor mathematical engine whatsoever, requires so much reparation as a woman's face.

*Duchess of Malfi* I. 1: I would, then, have a mathematical instrument made for her face. [*]

(f) Notice in the following passages the juxtaposition of ' dream ' and 'methought':

*Westward Ho* I. 1: I dreamed last night you looked so prettily, so sweetly, methought so like the wisest lady of them all.

*White Devil* V. 3: Wilt thou believe me, sweeting? by this light,
I was a-dreamt on thee, too; for methought
I saw thee . . .
FRANCISCO. Yes, and for fashion's sake I'll dream with her.
ZANCHE. Methought, sir, you came stealing to my bed . . .
ZANCHE. As I told you,
Methought you lay down by me.
FRANCISCO. So dreamt I.

*Duchess of Malfi* III. 5: DUCH. I had a very strange dream tonight. ANTONIO. What was it? DUCH. Methought I wore my coronet of state.

(g) *Westward Ho* I. 1: JUST. Painting, painting.
BIRD. I have of all sorts, forsooth: here is the burned powder of a hog's jawbone, to be laid with the oil of white poppy, an excellent fucus to kill morphew, weed out freckles, and a most excellent groundwork for painting; here is ginimony likewise burned and pulverized, to be mingled with the juice of lemons, sublimate mercury, and two spoonfuls of the flowers of brimstone, a most excellent receipt to cure the flushing in the face.

*Duchess of Malfi* II. 1 : You come from painting now . . . One would suspect it [your closet] for a shop of witchcraft, to find in it the fat of serpents, spawn of snakes, Jews' spittle, and their young children's ordure; and all these for the face.

(h) *Westward Ho* I. 1 : Love a woman for her tears! Let a man love oysters for their water: for women, though they should weep liquor enough to serve a dyer or a brewer, yet they may be as stale as wenches that travel every second tide between Gravesend and Billingsgate.

*Appius and Virginia* III. 2 : Of all waters, I would not have my beef powdered with a widow's tears . . . They are too fresh, madam; assure yourself, they will not last for the death of fourteen husbands above a day and a quarter.

*White Devil* V. 3 :

> These are but moonish shades of grief and fears;
> There's nothing sooner dry than women's tears.

(i) *Westward Ho* I. 1 : Just.   Ay, ay, provoking resistance; 'tis as if you come to buy wares in the city, bid money for't; your mercer or goldsmith says, "Truly I cannot take it," lets his customer pass his stall, next, nay, perhaps two or three; but if he find he is not prone to return of himself, he calls him back, and back, and takes his money: so you, my dear wife,—O the policy of women and tradesmen! they'll bite at anything.

*White Devil* I. 2 : Flamineo.   'Bove merit!—we may now talk freely—'bove merit! What is't you doubt? her coyness? that's but the superficies of lust most women have: yet why should ladies blush to hear that named which they do not fear to handle? Oh, they are politic: they know our desire is increased by the difficulty of enjoying, whereas satiety is a blunt, weary and drowsy passion.

(j) *Westward Ho* I. 1 : Mrs. Just.   Would you have me turn common sinner, or sell my apparel to my waistcoat and become a laundress? Just.   No laundress, dear wife, though your credit would go far with gentlemen for taking up of linen; no laundress.

*White Devil* III. 2:

> Did I want
> Ten leash of courtezans, it would furnish me;
> Nay, laundress three armies.

*Devil's Law Case* I. 2: [ROMELIO to WINIFRED]

> You, lady of the laundry, come hither.   [?]

(k) *Westward Ho* I. 1: Do not send me any letters; do not seek any reconcilement; by this light, I'll receive none . . . I hope we shall ne'er meet more.

*White Devil* II. 1:

> Henceforth, I'll never lie with you, by this,
> This wedding ring, I'll ne'er more lie with thee,
> And this divorce shall be as truly kept
> As if in thronged court a thousand ears
> Had heard it.   [?]

(l) *Westward Ho* I. 1: JUST.  Put case that this night-cap be too little for my ears or forehead.  Can any man tell me where my night-cap wrings me, except I be such an ass to proclaim it?

*White Devil* I. 2: CAM.  Come, you know not where my night-cap wrings me.  FLAM.  Wear it o' the old fashion; let your large ears come throngh.   [*]


## Mixed Passages.

The following passages show umistakable traces of Dekker, and some possible suggestions of Webster also:

(a) *Westward Ho* I. 1: Wear their hats o'er their eyebrows like politic penthouses, which commonly make the shop of a mercer or a linen-draper as dark as a room in Bedlam.

Dekker's *Peace is Broken*, p. 137: The mercers swore by their maidenhead that all their politic penthouses should be clothed in cloth of silver.

*Honest Whore II* I. 3:

> Not like a draper's shop with bold, dark shed.

*Duchess of Malfi* I. 1 :
> This darkening of your worth is not like that
> Which tradesmen use in the city; their false lights
> Are to rid bad wares off.

(b) *Westward Ho* I. 1 : Name you any one thing that your citizen's wife comes short of to your lady : they have as pure linen, as choice painting, love green-goose in spring, mallard and teal in the fall, and woodcock in winter.

Webster's *Devil's Law Case* I. 1 :
> Who is a woman of that state and bearing, ·
> Though she be city-born, both in her language,
> Her garments, and her table, she excels
> Our ladies of the court.

Dekker's *Gull's Hornbook*, chap. 1 : And according to the time of year vary your fare; as capon is a stirring meat sometimes, oysters are a swelling meat sometimes, trout a tickling meat sometimes, green goose and woodcock a delicate meat sometimes.

*Honest Whore II* III. 3 : We have poulterer's ware for your sweet bloods, as dove, chicken, duck, teal, woodcock, and so forth.

*Sun's Darling* IV : HUMOR.
> Into the court of winter; there thy food
> Shall not be sickly fruits, but healthful broths,
> Strong meat and dainty.

FOLLY. Pork, beef, mutton, very sweet mutton, veal, venison, capon, fine, fat capon, partridge, snipe, plover, larks, teal, admirable teal, my lord.

## Passages wholly from Dekker.

(a) *Westward Ho* I. 1 : How long will you hold out, think you? not so long as Ostend.

*Honest Whore I* IV. 1 : Indeed, that is harder to come by than ever was Ostend. [*]

(b) *Westward Ho* I. 1. Opportunity, which most of you long for (though you never be with child), opportunity.

*Roaring Girl* II. 1 : Why, 'tis but for want of opportunity thou knowest. — I put her off with opportunity still . . . I rail upon opportunity still and take no notice on't.

(c) *Westward Ho* I. 1: Just when women and vintners are a-conjuring, at midnight.

*Match Me in London* I. 1:

>The dawn of midnight and the drunkard's noon,
>No honest souls up now but vintners, midwives.

>>III:

>>Though they stand as low

>As vintners when they conjure.

(d) *Westward Ho* I. 1: You married me from the service of an honorable lady, and you know what matches I mought have had. What would you have me to do? I would I had never seen your eyes, your eyes.

*Bachelor's Banquet*, p. 165: Now cursed be the day that ever I saw thy face, and a shame take them that first brought me acquainted with thee . . . Was ever woman of my degree and birth brought to this beggary? Or any of my bringing up kept thus basely, and brought to this shame? . . . Whereas I might have had twenty good marriages.

Chap. 9, p. 239: Here his wife begins again to thwart him, 'Why, what would you have him do? It is impossible for any one to please you. . . . What would you have?'

*Roaring Girl* [underplot] II. 1: Mrs. O. 'Tis well known he took me from a lady's service, where I was well beloved of the steward.

*Conclusion.* When we remember how much more the same number of equally good passages count from Webster than from Dekker, we see that Webster must have written by far the larger part of this scene, although both poets unquestionably had a hand in it. These results agree with the results of the word-test, since the word-average of this scene is not high for Webster, but is far above Dekker's range.

Act I, Scene 2.
(130 solid lines; word-average, .215)
Passages from Webster.

(a) *Westward Ho* I. 2 : Thou art fain to take all and pay all.
*Devil's Law Case* III. 1 :

> And as your Dutch women in the Low Countries
> Take all and pay all.

(b) *Westward Ho* I. 2 : In troth, for the shaking of the heart: I have here sometimes such a shaking, and downwards such a kind of earth-quake, as it were.
*Appius and Virginia* V. 2 :

> What do you call
> A burning fever? is not that a devil?
> It shakes me like an earthquake. [?]

Passages from Dekker.

(a) *Westward Ho* I. 2 : Monopoly. Let me see the bond, let me see when this money is to be paid: the tenth of August, the first day that I must tender this money, is the first of dog-days.

*The Devil is in It*, p. 315 : Let me, before I swear, on my notes look, I'll tell you the very day ... The day, August 14th.

*Rod for Runaways*, p. 300 : A woman going along Barbican in the month of July, on a Wednesday, the first of the dog-days.

*Scrivener*. I fear 'twill be hot staying for you in London then.

*Raven's Almanac*. The Epistle [speaking to spendthrift gallants]: Read you only the dogdays of this Almanac, for when the sun entereth into Leo,... you shall find it will be exceeding hot walking up and down Fleet Street or Holborne.

(b) *Westward Ho* I. 2 : He will follow me when he thinks I have money, and pry into me as crows perch upon carrion.

*The Peace is Broken,* p. 119 : Young gentlemen that neither durst walk up and down the city, for fear of ravens and kites that hovered to catch them in their talons.

*Rod for Runaways,* p. 301 : Albeit all fled from her when she lived, yet, being dead, some like ravens seized upon her body.

*Lanthorn and Candlelight,* p. 257 : But ravens think carrion the daintiest meat.

*Conclusion.* The word-average of this scene is .215, an average which would not absolutely prohibit a large share for Webster, but which would create a strong presumption that Dekker wrote most of it. The parallel passages are a little uncertain. If the first one frrom Webster is not a proverb, it is close; but it sounds like a proverbial expression, and, if so, might be used by Dekker. The second parallel from Webster is not close, yet it has a certain likeness. On the whole, the passage-test seems to imply that both authors had a share in this scene, and that their relative parts are uncertain.

## Act II, Scene 1.
### (242 solid lines; word-average, .169).
### No passages from Webster.
### Passages from Dekker.

(a) *Westward Ho* II. 1 : If she be a right citizen's wife, now her husband has given her an inch, she'll take an ell, or a yard at least.

*Honest Whore II* II. 2 : Remember you're a linen draper, and that if you give your wife a yard, she'll take an ell... For if you take a yard, I'll take an ell. [*]

(b) *Westward Ho* II. 1 : I'm as limber as an ancient that has flourished in the rain, and as active as a Norfolk tumbler.

*Raven's Almanac*, p. 173. Yet are they of the nature of dogs and more nimble than Norfolk tumblers.

(*c̄*) *Westward Ho* II. 1: And *que nouvelles?* what news flutters abroad? Do jackdaws dung the top of Paul's steeple still?

*Satiro-mastix*, p. 194: Come, what news, what news abroad? I have heard of the horses walking a' the top of Paul's.

*News from Hell*, p. 131: They will flutter about him, crying, "What news, what news?"

(d) *Westward Ho* II. 1: [Speaks of Charing Cross as] The poor, wry-necked monument.

*Dead Term*: [London's answer to Westminster, speaks of Charing Cross as] That aged and reverend but wry-necked son of thine.

(e) *Westward Ho* II. 1: I had not thought, Master Parenthesis, you had been such an early stirrer.

*Shoemaker's Hol.* II. 3: O master, good-morrow; y'are an early stirrer.

*Satiro-mastix*, p. 189: You are an early stirrer, Sir Quintilian Shorthose.

(f) *Westward Ho* II. 1: But we ... must be up with the lark, because, like country attorneys, we are to shuffle up many matters in a forenoon.

*7 Deadly Sins*, p. 51: All are as busy as country attorneys at an assises.

(g) *Westward Ho* II. 1: Marry, because the suburbs, and those without the bars, have more privilege than they within the freedom.

*7 Deadly Sins*, p. 27: These [bankrupts, &c.] are indeed (and none but these) the foreigners that live without the freedom of your city better than you within it.

(h) *Westward Ho* II. 1: Her double F of a good length, but that it straddles a little too wide.

*News from Hell*, p. 94: The master of perdition would

by no means take them [lawyer's clerks] from their wide lines, and bursten bellied, straddling ff's.

(i) *Westward Ho* II. 1 : I am so troubled with the rheum, too.
*Honest Whore II* II. 1 : I'm an old man, sir, and am troubled with a whoreson salt rheum.

(j) *Westward Ho* II. 1 : Good Cole, tarry not past eleven.
*Honest Whore II* IV. 1 : Say no more, old Coal.
*Satiro-mastix*, p. 201 : Sayst thou me so, old Coal, come.

(k) *Westward Ho* II. 1 : JUST. Is he departed? Is old Nestor marched into Troy? M. HONEY. Yes, you mad Greek, the gentleman's gone.
*Shoemaker's Hol.* II. 3 : Here, Hodge, here, Firk; drink, you mad Greeks, and work like true Trojans.
*Fortunatus* III. 2 : These English occupiers are mad Trojans.
*Shoemaker's Hol.* III. 5 : Now, my true Trojans, my fine Firk.

(l) *Westward Ho* II. 1 : There's other irons in the fire; more sacks are coming to the mill.
*Bellman of London*, p. 152 [The Sacking Law.] : Sacks come to these mills every hour, but the sacking law empties them faster than a miller grinds his bushels of corn.

(m) *Westward Ho* II. 1 : See what golden-winged bee from Hybla flies humming with *crura thymo plena*, which he will empty in the hive of your bosom.
*Whore of Babylon*, p. 229 :
                 Only to employ them
As bees, whilst they have stings and bring thighs laden
With honey, hive them.

(n) *Westward Ho* II. 1 : Were I the properest, sweetest, plumpest, cherry-cheeked, coral lipped woman in a kingdom.
*Honest Whore I* II. 1 : She is the prettiest, kindest, sweetest, most bewitching honest ape under the pole.
*The Devil is in It*, p. 332 :
            Will you have a dainty girl, here 'tis;
            Coral lips, teeth of pearl, here 'tis;
            Cherry cheeks, softest flesh, that's she.

(o) *Westward Ho* II. 1 : Were I a poet, by Hippocrene I swear (which was a certain well where all the muses watered), and by Parnassus eke I swear, I would rhyme you to death with praises.

*Satiro-mastix*, p. 263 : By Apollo, Helicon, the Muses, (who march three and three in a rank) and by all that belongs to Parnassus, I swear all this.

(p) *Westward Ho* II. 1 : Men and women are born and come running into the world faster than coaches do into Cheapside upon Simon and Jude's day.

*Raven's Almanac* [Autumn]: Upon the very next day after Simon and Jude, the warlike drum and fife shall be heard in the very midst of Cheapside, at the noise whereof the people like madmen shall throng together, and run up and down.

*The Devil is in It,* p. 268:

> Were you good hell-hounds, every day should be
> A Simon and Jude, to crown our board with feasts
> Of black-eyed souls each miuute ; were you honest devils
> Each officer in hell should have at least
> A brace of whores to his breakfast . . .

OMNES. We'll fill thy palace with them.

(q) *Westward Ho* II. 1 : This world is like a mint . . . the old cracked King Harry groats are shovelled up, feel bruising and battering, chipping and melting, — they smoke for't.

*The Devil is in It*, p. 298 : BAR. Do not your gallants come off roundly then ? BRA. Yes sir, their hair comes off fast enough, we turn away crack't French crowns every day.

(r) *Westward Ho* II. 1 : The new money, like a new drab, is catched at by Dutch, Spanish, Welsh, French, Scotch, and English.

*Honest Whore I* II. 1 :

> A harlot is like Dunkirk, true to none,
> Swallows both English, Spanish, fulsome Dutch,
> Back-doored Italian, last of all, the French.

*Roaring Girl* V. 1: More countries to you than the Dutch, Spanish, French, or English ever found out.

*Honest Whore II* I. 1: There's a saying when they commend nations. It goes, the Irishman for his hand, the Welshman for a leg, the Englishman for a face, the Dutchman for a beard ... The Spaniard, — let me see, — for a little foot, I take it; the Frenchman, — what a pox hath he? and so of the rest.

*Peace is Broken*, p. 103: They were more scattered than the Jews and more hated, more beggarly than the Irish and more uncivil, more hardy than the Switzers, and more brutish, given to drink more than the Dutch, to pride more than the French, to irreligion more than the Italian.

*Match Me in London* III. p. 180:

> I do speak English
> When I'd move pity, when dissemble, Irish,
> Dutch when I reel, and though I feed on scalions
> If I should brag gentility I'd gabble Welsh,
> If I betray I'm French, if full of braves,
> They swell in lofty Spanish, in neat Italian
> I court my wench.

(s) *Westward Ho* II. 1: Why, even now ... some are murdering, some lying with their maids, some picking of pockets, some cutting purses, some cheating, some weighing out bribes; in this city some wives are cuckolding some husbands; in yonder village some farmers are now—now grinding the jawbones of the poor.

*Dead Term* [Westminster's complaint to London]: More maidenheads, I verily believe, are cut off upon my own featherbeds in one year than are heads of cattle cut off in two amongst the butchers that serve my families. . . . Other sins lie gnawing like diseases at my heart, for Pride sits at the doors of the rich: Envy goes up and down with the beggar, feeding upon snakes: rents are laid upon the rack even [in] my own sight and by my own children that I have borne, whilst Conscience goes like a fool in pied colors . . . Covetousness hath got a hundred hands, and all those hands

do nothing but tie knots on her purse-strings; but Prodigality
having but two hands, undoes those knots faster than the
other can tie them.

*The Devil is in It*, p. 268:

PLUTO. Is not the world as 't was?
  Once mother of rapes, incests, and sodomies,
  Atheism and blasphemies, plump boys indeed,
  That sucked our dam's breast, is she now barren? Ha!
  Is there a dearth of villanies?
OMNES. More now than ever.
PLUTO. Is there such penury of mankind hell-hounds,
  You can lie snoring?
BUFF. Each land is full of rake-hells.

(t) *Westward Ho* II. 1: A rare schoolmaster for all kinds
of hands, I.

*News from Hell*, p. 94: Whither then marches Mon. Male-
fico? Marry, to all the writing schoolmasters of the town.
He took them by the fists and liked their hands exceedingly
(for some of them had ten or twelve several hands, and
could counterfeit anything.)

(u) *Westward Ho* II. 1:

Well, if, as ivy 'bout the elm does twine,
All wives love clipping, there's no fault in mine.

*Batchelor's Banquet*, p. 264: Even so an old woman, having
gotten a young man, will cling to him, like an ivy to an elm. [*]

(v) *Westward Ho* II. 1: Even now must you and I hatch
an egg of iniquity.

*Lanthorn and Candlelight*, p. 267: She is the cockatrice
that hatcheth all these eggs of evils.

### Act II, Scene 2.
(270 solid lines; word-average, .148).

### Passages from Webster.

The only possible parallel passage for this scene which
I have been able to find in Webster is the following:

*Westward Ho* II. 1 :

> I wonder lust can hang at such white hairs.

*White Devil* IV. 1 :

> Where my love and care
> Shall hang your wishes in my silver hair.

There are, however, three objections to accepting this as Webster's. In the first place, there are two or three passages in Dekker which bear a slight, though rather shadowy likeness :

*Honest Whore I* V. 2 :

> And happiness shall crown your silver hairs.

*Satiro-mastix*, p. 228 :

> And rorid clouds, being sucked into the air,
> When down they melt, hangs like fine silver hair.

In the second place, there are metrical objections against giving this speech to Webster. The line in question forms a whole speech in itself, and rimes with the last line of the preceding speech. Rime between speeches is very rare in Webster, and very common in Dekker.

In the third place, a single unsupported passage like this is always liable to be the result of mere chance, unless it is long or very close, and this is neither. So, on the whole, this certainly seems very slight evidence, when balanced with what can be accumulated on the other side.

### Passages from Dekker.

(a) *Westward Ho* II. 2 [first line of scene]: Her answer, talk in· music; will she come ?

*Honest Whore I* I. 2 [first line of scene]: How now, porter, will she come ?

(b) *Westward Ho* II. 2: Had it not been for a friend in a corner [takes *aqua-vitæ*], I had kicked up my heels.

*Bachelor's Banquet*, chap. X, p. 242 : Meanwhile, she hath a sweetheart in a corner.

*Satiro-mastix*, p. 234 : For this man at arms has paper in's belly, or some friend in a corner, or else he durst not be so crank.

*Shoemaker's Holiday* III. 3 : I will have some odd thing or other in a corner for you; I will not be your back friend.

(c) *Westward Ho* II. 2 : The jealous wittol, her husband, came, like a mad ox, bellowing in while I was there.

*Match Me.* IV :

> Tormiella's husband,
> The mad ox broken loose.

*Honest Whore I* I. 1 : If . . . he [Hippolito] should get loose again and like a mad ox toss my new black cloaks into the kennel.

(d) *Westward Ho* II. 2 : I'll make the yellow-hammer her husband know that there's a difference between a cogging bawd and an honest, motherly gentlewoman.

*Honest Whore II* V. 2 : O, Mistress Cathrine, you do me wrong to accuse me here as you do, before the right worshipful. I am known for a motherly, honest woman, and no bawd.[1]

(e) *Westward Ho* II. 2 : A woman when there be roses in her cheeks, cherries on her lips, civet in her breath, ivory in her teeth, lilies in her hand, and liquorice in her heart.

*The Devil is in It*, p. 332 :

> Will you have a dainty girl, here 'tis ;
> Coral lips, teeth of pearl. here 'tis ;
> Cherry cheeks, softest flesh, that's she.

(f) *Westward Ho* II. 2 : The whiting-mop has nibbled.

*Honest Whore II* III. 3 : She nibbled, but would not swallow the hook.

---

[1] Pointed out by Mr. Stoll.

*Whore of Babylon*, p. 234:
> Though you bait hooks with gold,
> Ten thousand may be nibbling.

*The Peace is Broken*, p. 120: If fat widows can be but drawn to nibble at that worshipful bait.

*Roaring Girl* II. 1: Heart, I would give but too much money to be nibbling with that wench.

(g) *Westward Ho* II. 2:
> This shower shall fill them all; rain in their laps
> What golden drops thou wilt.

*Fortunatus* III. 1:
> Unless he melt himself to liquid gold,
> Or be some god, some devil, or can transport
> A mint about him by enchanted power,
> He cannot rain such showers.

*Wonder of a Kingdom* III. p. 256:
> > Who bravely pours
> But into a wench's lap his golden showers,
> May be Jove's equal.

*Match Me in London* II. p. 164:
> The God of gold pour down on both your heads
> His comfortable showers.[1]

---

[1] Compare also the following from Webster:

*Duchess of Malfi* II. 2: If we have the same golden showers that rained in the time of Jupiter the thunderer, you have the same Danaës still, to hold up their laps to receive them.

*Duchess of Malfi* I, 1:

FERD. There's gold.
BOSOLA.                    So:
> What follows? never rained such showers as these
> Without thunderbolts i' the tail of them.

As the passage from *Fortunatus* was written before *Westward Ho*, and the *Duchess of Malfi* long after, it seems probable that Dekker wrote the passage in *Westward Ho*, and that the passages in the *Duchess of Malfi* are a trace of Dekker's influence on his younger, or at least, less experienced associate. It seems hardly probable that passages so close and numerous should be wholly due to chance, even allowing for the story of Danaë.

(h) *Westward Ho* II. 2: O, she looks so sugaredly, so simperingly, so gingerly, so amorously, so amiably! Such a red lip, such a white forehead, such a black eye, such a full cheek, and such a goodly little nose.

*Match Me in London* I: Delicate, piercing eye, enchanting voice, lip red and moist, skin soft and white; she's amorous, delicious, inciferous, tender, neat.

(i) *Westward Ho* II. 2: You shall not find him a Templar, nor one of these cogging Catherine-pear-colored beards.

*Honest Whore* I V. 2: My eldest son had a polt-foot, crooked legs, a verjuice face, and a pear-colored beard.

(j) *Westward Ho* II. 2: I think you'll find the sweetest, sweetest bedfellow of her.

*Wonder of a Kingdom* II: If Death do take her, he shall have the sweetest bedfellow that ever lay by lean man's side.

*Honest Whore* I III. 2: There's the finest, neatest gentleman at my house. ... There's the sweetest, properest, gallantest gentleman at my house.

*Honest Whore* II I. 1: Our country *buona-robas*, oh! are the sugarest, delicious rogues.

(k) *Westward Ho* II. 2: You shall see, I'll fetch her with a wet finger.

*Honest Whore* I I. 2: If ever I stand in need of a wench that will come with a wet finger.

*Honest Whore* I V. 1:

> For she'll pump water from her eyes
> With a wet finger. [*]

(l) *Westward Ho* II. 2: Now the marks are set up, I'll get me twelve score off and give aim.

*7 Deadly Sins* [Induction]: The English, the Dutch, and the Spanish stood aloof and gave aim, whilst thou [France] shotst arrows upright. [?]

(m) *Westward Ho* II. 2:

> I have already leaped beyond the bounds
> Of modesty, in piecing out my wings
> With borrowed feathers.

*Whore of Babylon*, p. 235:
The wings from home that brought me had sick feathers.
*Roaring Girl* IV. 2:
                    Husband, I plucked,
When he had tempted me to think well of him,
Gilt feathers from thy wings, to make him fly
More lofty.
(n) *Westward Ho* II. 2:
And henceforth cease to throw out golden hooks
To choke mine honour.
*Witch of Edmonton* IV. 1:
Dare any swear I ever tempted maiden
With golden hooks flung at her chastity.[1]
*Honest Whore I* II. 1:
                    And then a fourth
Should have this golden hook, and lascivious bait,
Thrown out to the full length.

*Fortunatus* I. 2:
This strumpet World; for her most beauteous looks
Are poisoned baits hung upon golden hooks.

*Wonder of a Kingdom* I: Bait a hook with gold and
with it . . . . .
*Whore of Babylon*, p. 217:
Such swelling spirits hid with humble looks,
Are kingdoms' poisons hung on golden hooks.

*Roaring Girl* III. 1:
MOLL. Such hungry things as these may soon be took
With a worm fastened on a golden hook.[1]

(o) *Westward Ho* II. 2:
                    Though my husband 's poor,
I'll rather beg for him than be your whore.
*Shoemaker's Holiday* IV. 1:
Whilst he lives, his I live, be it ne'er so poor,
And rather be his wife than a king's whore.

[1] These also throw some light on Dekker's part in *The Witch of Edmonton* and *The Roaring Girl.*

*Honest Whore II* II. 1:

> He loved me; being now poor,
> I'll beg for him, and no wife can do more.

*Match Me in London* II:

> What violent hands
> Soever force me, ne'er shall touch woman more,
> I'll kill ten monarchs ere I'll be one's whore.

III:

> I will not be your whore to wear your crown,
> Nor call any king my husband but mine own.

(p) *Westward Ho* II. 2:

> Thou art a very bawd, thou art a devil
> Cast in a reverend shape, thou stale damnation.

*Honest Whore I* III. 2:

> Hence, thou, our sex's monster, poisonous bawd,
> Lust's factor, and damnation's orator.

*I* II. 1:

> Why, those that love you, hate you, and will term you
> Liquorish damnation.

(q) *Westward Ho* II. 2: Is not old wine wholesomest, old pippins toothsomest, old wood burn brightest, old linen wash whitest? [*]

(1) Compare for the use of superlatives:

*Honest Whore I* III. 2: There's the sweetest, properest, gallantest gentleman at my house.

(2) Compare for the fourfold, balanced form of the sentence:

*The Peace is Broken*, p. 97: To walk every day into the fields is wearisome; to drink up the day and night in a tavern loathsome; to be ever riding upon the beast with two heads (Lechery) most damnable, and yet to be ever idle is detestable.

(r) *Westward Ho* II. 2: If new, very good company; but if stale, like old Jeronimo, go by, go by.

*Shoemaker's Holiday* II. 1 : But if I were as you, I'd cry :
    Go by, Jeronimo, go by.
*Satiro-mastix*, p. 202 : Go by, Jeronimo, go by; and here
drop the 10 shillings. [*]

(s) *Westward Ho* II. 2 : I see that, as Frenchmen love to
be bold, Flemings to be drunk, Welshmen to be called
Britons, and Irishmen to be costermongers, so cockneys,
especially she-cockneys love not *aqua-vitæ* when 'tis good
for them.
[For parallel passages see *Westward Ho*, II. 1 (r)].

(t) *Westward Ho* II. 2 : MRS. JUST. Witch, thus I break
thy spells.
*Wonder of a Kingdom* II :
    TIBALDO.        Against your charms,
        Witch, thus I stop mine ears.

(u) *Westward Ho* II. 2 : BIRDLIME. Here's a letter to your
worship from the party. MONOPOLY. What party ? BIRD. The
Tenterhook, your wanton.
*Wonder of a Kingdom* IV : GENTILI. What next ? SER-
VANT. The party, sir. GENTILI. What party, sir ?

(v) *Westward Ho* II. 2 : BIRDLIME. But shall not the party
be there ? MONOPOLY. Which party ? BIRDLIME. The writer
of that simple hand.
    [Compare with (u) above].

(w) *Westward Ho* II. 2 : From her ! phew ! pray thee,
stretch me no more upon your Tenterhook.
*Honest Whore II* IV. 2 : To make a piece of English cloth
of him, and to stretch him on the tenters, till the threads of
his own natural humor crack.
*Satiro-mastix*, p. 246 :
    Oh Night, that dyes the firmament in black,
    And like a cloth of clouds dost stretch thy limbs
    Upon the windy tenters of the air.
*Match Me in London* III :
        My urinalist . . . left no artery
        Unstretcht upon the tenters.

Act II, Scene 3.

(129 solid lines; word-average, . 155).

No passages from Webster.

Passages from Dekker.

(a) *Westward Ho* II. 3: Wine in the must, good Dutch-man, for must is best for us women.

*Satiro-mastix*, p. 247: Must is a king, and I must go.

*Patient Grisill*, p. 194: I must, must is for kings.   [?]

(b) *Westward Ho* II. 3: An honest butter-box.

*Shoemaker's Holiday* II. 3: We have not men enow, but we must entertain every butter-box.

III. 1: FIRK. They may well be called butterboxes when they drink fat veal and thick beer too.

*News from Hell*, p. 145: Those butterboxes, says Charon, [of the souls of two Dutchmen] owe me a penny.

(c) *Westward Ho* II. 3: HANS.   Yaw, yaw, you sall hebben it, mester.

*Shoemaker's Holiday* II. 3: LACY [as HANS].  Yaw, yaw, ik bin den shomawker . . . . Yaw, yaw; be niet vorveard . . . Yaw, yaw, yaw; ik can dat wel doen.

(d) *Westward Ho* II. 3: Bun, bun, bun, bun.

*Honest Whore I* II. 1: Down, down, down, down [?]

(e) *Westward Ho* II. 3: For he feeds thee with nothing but court holy-bread, good words, and cares not for thee.

*Match Me in London* III:

For you must think that all that bow, stand bare
And give court cake-bread to you, love you not.

(f) *Westward Ho* II. 3: Wo-ho, ho, ho, so-ho, boys.

*Match Me in London* I: Wo, ho, ho, ho, — whew.

*Fortunatus* I. 1: So, ho, ho, ho, ho.

*The Devil is in It*, p. 811: So, ho, ho, father subprior.

(g) *Westward Ho* II. 3: Who would not be scratched with the briers and brambles to have such burrs sticking on his breeches?

*Whore of Babylon*, p. 222: This burr still hangs on me.

*Wonder of Kingdom* II: But no point can peek out le remedie for de madam in de briers of love.[1] [?]

(h) *Westward Ho* II. 3: Oh Lord, oh gentlemen, knights, ladies that may be, citizens' wives that are, shift for your-selves, for a pair of your husbands' heads are knocking together with Hans his, and inquiring for you.

*Shoemaker's Holiday* IV. 4: Oh God, what will you do, mistress? Shift for yourself, your father is at hand. [?]

(i) *Westward Ho* II. 3: Sirrah, Wafer, thy child's at nurse: — if you that are the men could provide some wise ass that could keep his countenance; one that could set out his tale with audacity, and say that the child were sick, and ne'er stagger at it; that last should serve all our feet.

*Bachelor's Banquet,* chap. 8: After this agreement, home she comes with a heavy countenance: the good man asketh what she aileth. Marry, quoth she, the child is very ill at ease (though he was never in better health since he was born), his flesh burns as though it were fire; and, as the nurse tells me, he hath refused the dug these two days, although she durst not say so much till now.

*Roaring Girl* III. 2: [Gallipot to his wife] Is not thy child at nurse fallen sick or dead?


## Act III, Scene 1.
### (52 solid lines; word average, .250)
### No passages from Webster.
### Passages from Dekker.

(a) *Westward Ho* III. 1: MRS. TENTERHOOK.   No, lamb. [Exit Tenterhook.]   Baa, sheep.

---

[1] Compare also the following from Webster:
*White Devil* V. 1:
> Women are like to burrs,
> Where their affection throws them, there they'll stick.

The *Whore of Babylon* was almost certainly written before the *White Devil*; and, on the whole, Dekker's claim seems stronger. If this likeness is more than mere chance, it may be a trace of Dekker's literary influence on his younger companion.

*Honest Whore I* V. 2 : MAT. Yes, lamb. BELL. Baa, lamb.[1]

(b) *Westward Ho* III. 1 : Well, my husband is gone to arrest Monopoly; I have dealt with a sergeant privately, to entreat him, pretending that he is my aunt's son: by this means shall I see my young gallant that in this has played his part. When they owe money in the city once, they deal with their lawyers by attorney, follow the court, though the court do them not the grace to allow them their diet.

*Roaring Girl* IV. 2 : Then deal they [our gallants] underhand with us; . . . and we must swear they are our cousins, and able to do us a pleasure at court.

## Act III, Scene 2.
### (112 solid lines; word-average, .234).
### Passage from Webster.

*Westward Ho* III. 2 : MON. Thou hast backed many a man in thy time, I warrant. AMB. I have had many a man by the back, sir.

*Appius and Virginia* III. 2 : 1ST LICT. We back knights and gentlemen daily. 2ND. LICT. Right, we have them by the back hourly.

### Passages from Dekker.

(a) *Westward Ho* III. 2 : AMB. Phew, I have been a broker already; for I was first a Puritan, then a bankrupt, then a broker, then a fencer, and then sergeant: were not these trades would make a man honest?

*Patient Grissil* III. 1 : BABULO. At first I was a fool, for I was born an innocent; then I was a traveler, and then a basketmaker, and then a courtier, and now I must turn basketmaker and fool again.

(b) *Westward Ho* III. 2 : Now were I in an excellent humor to go to a vaulting house: I would break down all their glass windows, hew in pieces all their joint-stools, tear

---

[1] Pointed out by Stoll.

their silk petticoats, ruffle their periwigs, and spoil their painting.

*Patient Grissil* IV. 3: [Gwenthyan to Sir Owen] No, our lord is mad: you tear her ruffs and repatoes and pridle her: is her pridled now? is her repatoed now? is her tear in pieces now?

(c) *Westward Ho* III. 2; As you are a gentleman, lend me forty shillings: let me not live if I do not pay you the forfeiture of the whole bond, and never plead conscience.

*Lanthorn and Candlelight*, p. 256: Make me, sir, so much beholden to your love as to lend me forty or fifty shillings to bear myself and my horse to London; from whence within a day or two, I shall send you many thanks with a faithful repayment of your courtesy.

*Honest Whore I* I. 2: Marry, I must entreat you to lend me some thirty or forty till the ship come: by this hand, I'll discharge at my day, by this hand.

(d) *Westward Ho* III. 2: You shall have my sword and hangers to pay him.

*Honest Whore II* IV. 1: An excellent gilt rapier . . . I could feast ten good fellows with these hangers. [?]

### Act III, Scene 3.
#### (132 solid lines; word-average, .333).

#### Passages from Webster.

(a) *Westward Ho* III. 3: The commonest sinner had more fluttering about her than a fresh punk hath when she comes to a town of garrison or to a university.

*Duchess of Malfi* II. 5:

> She hath had most cunning bawds to serve her turn,
> And more secure conveyances for lust
> Than towns of garrison for service.

(b) *Westward Ho* III. 3: There is a great strife between beauty and chastity; and that which pleaseth many is never free from temptation.

*White Devil* III. 1 :

> Grant I was tempted:
> Temptation to lust proves not the act:
> *Casta est quam nemo rogavit.* [?]

(c) *Westward Ho* III. 3: Why, your Italians in general, are so burnt with these dog-days, that your great lady there thinks her husband loves her not, if he be not jealous.

*Duchess of Malfi* I. 1: Blackbirds fatten best in hard weather; why not I in these dog-days?

*White Devil* II. 1: My jealousy! I am yet to learn what that Italian means.

> *Cure for a Cuckold* V. 1:
> Are you returned
> With the Italian plague upon
> you, jealousy?

(d) *Westward Ho* III. 3: What an idle coxcomb jealousy will make a man . . . As for jealousy, it makes many cuckolds, many fools, and many bankrupts; it may have abused me, and not my wife's honesty; I'll try it.

*White Devil* I. 2: It seems you would be a fine capricious mathematically jealous coxcomb; . . . they that have the yellow jaundice think all objects that they look on to be yellow. Jealousy is worser; her fits present to a man, like so many bubbles in a bason of water, twenty several crabbed faces; many times makes his shadow his cuckold-maker . . . This is all; be wise, I will make you friends.

*White Devil* II. 1:

> Now, by my birth, you are a foolish, mad,
> And jealous woman.

*Note.* The two following passages are given, not for particular phrases, but for general style, and not as proof, but as refutation. Too many people think that the mere mention of a Dutchman, or a list of low-life characters, proves Dekker's authorship.

(e) *Westward Ho* III. 3: Captains, scholars, servingmen, jurors, clerks, townsmen, and the black guard used all one ordinary.

*White Devil* II. 2:

> But what a piteous cry there straight arose
> Amongst smiths and feltmakers, brewers and cooks,
> Reapers and butterwomen, amongst fishmongers,
> And thousand other trades [?]

(†) *Westward Ho* III. 3: Looking as pitifully as Dutchmen first made drunk.

*Appius and Virginia* IV. 2:

> Though we dine to-day
> As Dutchmen feed their soldiers.

*White Devil* III. 1:

> An unbidden guest
> Should travel as Dutchwomen go to church.

*Devil's Law Case* III. 1: And as your Dutchwomen in the Low Countries [?]

### Passage from Dekker.

*Westward Ho* III. 3: You shall not hit me in the teeth that I was your hindrance.

*Bachelor's Banquet*, p. 158: Jesus God, saith she, when you have nothing else to hit in the teeth withal, ye twit me with the tenement.

*Roaring Girl* IV, 2: Presently I hit him in the teeth with the Three Pigeons.

*Satiro-Mastix*, p. 196: One hit me in the teeth that the greatest clerks are not the wisest men.

*Patient Grissil* III. 1: He shall never hit us in the teeth with turning us, for 'tis not a good turn.[1]

*Virgin Martyr* II. 1: The ... page hit me in the teeth with it.[1]

*Conclusion.* It seems clear that both writers had a hand in this scene, and also that Webster had the larger part. It should be noticed that the one parallel from Dekker comes in the short dialogue of the Wafers, during which Justiniano is almost wholly silent. Now compare this fact with the word-test for this scene:

---

[1] The last two parallels were pointed out by Bangs, *Eng. Stud.*, Vol. 28.

| *Westward Ho* III. 3. | Solid lines. | Words. | Average. |
|---|---|---|---|
| Boy | 5 | 2 | |
| Justiniano | 106 | 38 | . 358 |
| Wafer | 6 | 1 | . 166 |
| Mrs. Wafer | 15 | 3 | . 200 |

Of course, the word-test here did not prove that Dekker wrote the dialogue of the Wafers; for the word-test becomes unreliable when applied to such small units; but it agrees beautifully with such a theory when indicated by another test.

Act III, Scene 4.
(65 solid lines; word-average, . 215)
No Passages from Webster.

Passages from Dekker.

(a) *Westward Ho* III. 4: Come, because I kept from town a little, — let me not live if I did not hear the sickness was in town very hot.

*Rod for Runaways*, p. 289: He, being determined to retire into the country, sent for some of the better sort of his neighbours, asked their good wills to leave them, and because (the poison of the pestilence so hotly reigning) he knew not whether they and he should ever meet again.

p. 297: The heat of contagion frights them from returning, and it were a shame, they think, to come so soon back to that city.

(b) *Westward Ho* III. 4: Because women's tongues are like to clocks; if they go too fast, they never go true.

*News from Hell*, p. 106: But their wits, like wheels in Brunswick clocks, being all wound up, so far as they could stretch, were all going, but not one going truly.

*Honest Whore II* III. 1: INF. Mine [watch] goes by heaven's dial, the sun, and it goes true.

HIP. I think, indeed, mine runs somewhat too fast.

Act IV, Scene 1.

(242 solid lines; word-average, .169)

No passages from Webster.

Passages from Dekker.

(a) *Westward Ho* IV. 1: Birdlime. God send me deuces and aces with a court-card, and I shall get by it. Honeysuckle. That can make thee nothing. Birdlime. Yes, if I have a coat-card turn up.

*Match Me in London* IV: I did but shuffle the first dealing; you cut last and dealt last; by the same token you turned up a court-card.

(b) *Westward Ho* IV. 1: What, more sacks to the mill! I'll to my old retirement.

*Bellman of London*, p. 152 [The Sacking Law]: Sacks come to these mills every hour.

(c) *Westward Ho* IV. 1: You went to a butcher's feast at Cuckold's Haven the next day after St. Luke's day.

*Match Me* I: If she should drive you by foul weather into Cuckold's Haven before St. Luke's day comes.

*News from Hell*, p. 98: May you sail sooner thither than a married man can upon St. Luke's day to Cuckold's Haven.

*Raven's Almanac* [Winter]: And sithence upon St. Luke's day, bitter storms of wind and hail are likely to happen about Cuckold's Haven.

(d) *Westward Ho* IV. 1: Loves, well, would you knew what I know! then you would say somewhat. In good faith, she's very poor: all her gowns are at pawn; she owes me five pound for her diet, besides forty shillings I lent her to redeem two half-silk kirtles from the broker's: and do you think she would be in debt thus, if she thought not of somebody?

*Honest Whore* I III. 1: I would thou wouldst give me five yards of lawn, to make my punk some falling bands

a' the fashion; three falling one upon another, for that's
the new edition now: she's out of linen horribly, too; troth,
sh'as never a good smock to her back neither, but one that
has a great many patches in't.

(e) *Westward Ho* IV. 1: BIRDLIME.    Say that you were
a country gentleman, or a citizen that hath a young wife,
or an Inn of Chancery man, should I tell you? pardon me.

*Gull's Hornbook*, chap. 7: Whether he be a country
gentleman that brings his wife up to learn the fashion, see
the tombs at Westminster, the lions in the Tower, or to
take physic; or else some young farmer, who many times
makes his wife in the country believe he hath suits in law
because he will come up to his lechery.


### Act IV, Scene 2.
(202 solid lines: word-average, .149).

No passages from Webster.

Passages from Dekker.

(a) *Westward Ho* IV. 2 [Opening lines of scene]:
EARL.    Have you perfumed the chamber?
OMNES.    Yes, my lord.
*Wonder of a Kingdom* III [Opening lines of scene]:
TORRENTI.    This room smells.    1ST GALLANT.    It has been
new perfumed.

(b) *Westward Ho* IV. 2:
> Go, let music
> Charm with her excellent voice an awful silence
> Through all this building, that her sphery soul
> May, on the wings of air, in thousand forms
> Invisibly fly, yet be enjoyed.

*Fortunatus* I. 1:
> Take instruments,
> And let the raptures of choice harmony,
> Thorough the hollow windings of his ear,
> Carry their sacred sound, and wake each sense,
> To stand amazed at our bright eminence.

*The Peace is Broken*, p. 125: When music went into her ear in ten thousand several shapes.

(e) *Westward Ho* IV. 2: 1ST SERV. Does my lord mean to conjure, that he draws these strange characters?
2ST SERV. He does; but we shall see neither the spirit that rises, nor the circle it rises in.

*Lanthorn and Candlelight*, p. 262: If any passenger come by, and, wondering to see such a conjuring circle kept by hellhounds, demand what spirits they raise there . . .

*Whore of Babylon*, p. 242: It's the maddest circle to conjure in that ever raised spirit.

*Match Me in London* IV:

> Look all, bind fast this devil, is there no circle
> To be damned in but mine?

*Ibid.* V: Wilt thou help me to a fit circle to play the devil in? [*]

(d) *Westward Ho* IV. 2: By scorching her with the hot stream of lust.

*The Peace is Broken*, p. 100: I left swimming in those common sensual streams, wherein the world hath been so often in danger of being drowned.

(e) *Westward Ho* IV. 2: Hard was the siege which you laid to the crystal walls of my chastity, but I held out, you know.

*Honest Whore II* IV. 1:

> I'll try
> If now I can beat down this chastity
> With the same ordnance; will you yield this fort?

*Wonder of a Kingdom* I: Her walls of chastity cannot be beaten down.

*Wonder of a Kingdom* II: As for my old huckster's artillery, I have walls of chastity strong enough, shoot he never so hard.

(f) *Westward Ho* IV. 2:

> I begged that she would die; my suit was granted;
> I poisoned her; thy lust there strikes her dead.

*Satiro-mastix*, p. 252 :

> Ask the king that; he was the cause, not I.
> Let it suffice, she's dead, she kept her vow.

(g) *Westward Ho* IV. 2 : But to pare off these brims [horns].
*Fortunatus* V. 1 : Thrice have we pared them off.
*Honest Whore II* I. 3 : The seaman has his cap, pared without brim.

(h) *Westward Ho* IV. 2 :

> Mirror of dames, I look upon thee now,
> As men long blind, having recover'd sight,
> Amazed, scarce able to endure the light.
> Mine own shame strikes me dumb: henceforth the book
> I'll read shall be thy mind and not thy look.

*Satiro-mastix*, p. 255 :

> Do not confound me quite; for mine own guilt
> Speaks more within me than thy tongue contains;
> Thy sorrow is my shame: yet herein springs
> Joy out of sorrow, boldness out of shame;
> For I by this have found, once in my life,
> A faithful subject, thou a constant wife.
> . . . Mirror of maidens, wonder of thy name.

*Roaring Girl* IV. 2 : Mine own shame me confounds.
*Whore of Babylon*, p. 264 :

> Mirror of women,
> I open now my breast even to the heart.

(i) *Westward Ho* IV. 2 : The book of the siege of Ostend, written by one that dropped in the action, will never sell so well as a report of the siege between this grave, this wicked elder and thyself.

*Honest Whore I* IV. 1 : Indeed, that's harder to come by than ever was Ostend.

*Satiro-mastix*, p. 218 : Hark, hither, Susanna, beware of these two wicked elders.

(j) *Westward Ho* IV. 2 : The moon's up : 'fore Don Phœbus, I doubt we shall have a frost this night, her horns are so sharp.

*The Devil is in It,* p. 310: Look you, because the moon is up and makes horns at one of us.

*Match Me in London* I:
> Do you see this change in the moon? Sharp horns
> Do threaten windy weather.

## Act V, Scene 1.
### (270 solid lines; word-average, .200)
### No passages from Webster.
### Passages from Dekker.

*Westward Ho* V. 1: And then he sets out a throat and swore again like a stinking-breathed knight as he was, that women were like horses ... They'd break over any hedge to change their pasture, though it were worse.

*Dead Term* [London's answer]: Such is the quality of Smithfield nags, such is the property of suburb courtesans. In brief, their beginning is bravery, their end beggary, their life is detestable, and death, for the most part, damnable.

*The Peace is Broken,* p. 109: If they were taken wandering, like sheep broken out of lean pastures into fat, out of their own liberties.

(b) *Westward Ho* V. 1: I know what one of 'em buzzed in mine ear, till, like a thief in a candle, he made mine ears burn.

*Match Me in London* I:
> Before he came, you buzzed into mine ear
> Tunes that did sound but scurvily.

*Bachelor's Banquet,* chap. 12, p. 256: About some odd errand which she will buzz in his ears.

*Roaring Girl* IV. 2: Some slave has buzzed this into her, has he not? [*]

(c) *Westward Ho* V. 1: I know as verily they hope and brag to one another, that this night they'll row westward in our husbands' wherries.

*Wonder of a Kingdom* I: Thou knowest the Donna Alphonsina ... is 't not a galley for the great Turk to be rowed in?

*Honest Whore I* V. 2:

> Must I sail in your fly-boat,
> Because I helped to rear your main-mast first?

[All three passages used in the same metaphorical sense.]

(d) *Westward Ho* V. 1: Be as wanton as new-married wives, as fantastic and light-headed to the eye as feather-makers, but as pure about the heart as if we dwelt amongst 'em in Blackfriars.

*Seven Deadly Sins* [V, Apishness]: He's a fierce, dapper fellow, more light-headed than a musician; as fantastically attired as a court jester; wanton in discourse; lascivious in behaviour; jocund in good company; nice in his trencher; and yet he feeds very hungerly on scraps of songs. [?]

(e) *Westward Ho* V. 2: [To be compared with the above] Oh yes; eat with 'em as hungerly as soldiers; drink as if we were froes; talk as freely as jesters; but do as little as misers, who, like dry nurses, have great breasts but give no milk. [?]

(f) *Westward Ho* V. 1: That he who shall miss his hen, if he be a right cock indeed, will watch the other from treading.

*Honest Whore II* V. 2: This is the hen, my lord, that the cock with the lordly comb, your son-in-law, would crow over, and tread.

*Roaring Girl* III. 2: 'T is one of Hercules' labours to tread one of these city hens, because their cocks are still crowing over them.

(g) *Westward Ho* V. 1: Ill, ill, ill, ill, ill.

*Fortunatus* V. 1: Fie, fie, fie, fie, . . . vel, vel, vel, vel, vel.

## Act V, Scene 3.[1]
(84 solid lines; word-average, .119)
No passages from Webster.
Passages from Dekker.

(a) *Westward Ho* V. 3: BIRDLIME. I ha' brought some women a-bed in my time, sir. SIR GOSLING. Ay, and some young men, too, hast not, Pandora?

*Wonder of a Kingdom* II: I'll swear all this stir is about having a woman brought to bed; marry, I doubt it must be a man's lying in.

(b) *Westward Ho* V. 3: Play, you lousy Hungarians.

*Bellman of London*, p. 83: The poor Hungarian answered, yes, he was.

*News from Hell*, p. 108: Only for my sake the lean jade Hungarian [his father, no slang term][2] would not lay out a penny pot of sack for himself.

### Compare also the following:

*Shoemaker's Holiday* II. 3: Come, you mad Hyperboreans ...
III. 1: Here you mad Mesopotamians ... Silk and satin, you mad Philistines ... V. 1: I promised the mad Cappadocians ... My fine, dapper Assyrian lads shall clap up their windows.

(c) *Westward Ho* V. 3: Play, life of Pharaoh, play.

*Shoemaker's Holiday* III. 1: By the life of Pharaoh, by the Lord of Ludgate ... V. 1: By the life of Pharaoh, by this beard ... I. 1: By the life of Pharaoh, a brave, resolute swordsman.

(d) *Westward Ho* V. 3: Sing, Madge, Madge: sing, owlet.

*Shoemaker's Holiday* III. 5: Come, Madge, on with your trinkets, ... Come, Madge, away, ... V. 1: Why, my sweet Lady Madgy, ... Lady Madgy, thou hadst never

---

[1] V. 2 in Dyce is merely eight lines of soliloquy.

[2] Dyce says this was a technical canting term; but the context in this passage shows that it has no technical use here. Whether as canting term or slang, it is one of a list of common Dekkerian expressions.

covered thy Saracen's head, ... Lady Madgy, Lady Madgy,
take two or three of my pie-crust eaters, ... Trip and go,
my Lady Madgy, ... III. 1 : No more, Madge, no more.

(e) *Westward Ho* V. 3 : How many of my name, of the Glow-
worms, have paid for your furred gowns, thou woman's broker ?

*Lanthorn and Candlelight*, p. 297: A company of grave
and wealthy lechers in the shapes of glow-worms, who
with gold jingling in their pockets made such a shew in
the night that the doors of common brothelries flew open
to receive them.

(f) *Westward Ho* V. 3 : BIRDLIME [to SIR G. GLOWWORM].
No sir, I scorn to be beholding to any glow-worm that lives
upon earth for my fur; I can keep myself warm without
glow-worms.

*Wonderful Year* [To the Reader]: How notoriously, therefore, do good wits dishonour, not only their calling, but even
their creation, that worship glow-worms instead of the sun
because of a little false glistering.[1]

(g) *Westward Ho* V. 3 : What kin art thou to Long Meg
of Westminster ? Thou'rt like her.

*Roaring Girl* V. 1 : Was it your Meg of Westminster's
courage that rescued me from the Poultry Puttocks indeed ?

*Satiro-mastix*, p. 219 : No, 't is thou mak'st me so, my
Long Meg a Westminster.

(h) *Westward Ho* V. 3 : Mary Ambree, do not you know me ?
*Satiro-mastix*, p. 221 : I say, Mary Ambree, thou shalt
march foremost.

(i) *Westward Ho* V. 3 : Cannot the shaking of the sheets[2]
be danced without your town piping ?

*Shoemaker's Holiday* IV. 5 : Shortly are to come over one
another with ' Can you dance the shaking of the sheets ? ' ...

---

[1] Compare with *Wonderful Year* (although it shows no likeness
to *Westward Ho*) Webster's famous lines :

> Glories, like glow-worms, afar off shine bright,
> But looked to near have neither heat nor light.

*White Devil* V. 1, and again in *Duchess of Malfi*.

[2] A stock pun, but a great favorite with Dekker, and never,
I think, used by Webster.

V. 5: I danced the shaking of the sheets with her six and thirty years ago.

*Satiro-mastix*, p. 208: You shall be put in among these ladies, and dance ere long, I trust, the shaking of the sheets. [*]

(j) *Westward Ho* V. 3 [Sɪʀ Gosʟɪɴɢ to Bɪʀᴅʟɪᴍᴇ]: Mary Ambree, do you not know me? ... Whither art bound, galley-foist? ... Whence comest thou, female yeoman of the guard? ... Dost come to keep the door, Ascapart? ... Hast not, Pandora? ... I would prove 'em, Mother Best-be-trust. ... Do I not, Megæra? ... Canst sing, woodpecker?

*Shoemaker's Holiday* [Sɪᴍᴏɴ Eʏʀᴇ to Mᴀʀɢᴇʀʏ]: Peace, pudding broth. ... Peace, you gallimafry. ... Is 't so, Dame Clapperdudgeon?... Trip and go, you soused conger, away!... Peace, you bombast-cotton-candle-quean; away, queen of clubs. ... Away, rubbish. ... Avaunt, kitchen-stuff! Rip, you brown-bread Tannikin. ... Look, you powder-beef-quean.... Rip, you chitterling, avaunt. ... Away, you Islington white-pot. ... Avaunt, avoid, Mephistophiles. ... Vanish, Mother Miniver-cap.

(k) *Westward Ho* V. 3: Fiddlers, come, strike up. ... You shall sing bawdy songs under every window i' the town; up will the clowns start, down come the wenches; we'll set the men a-fighting, the women a-scolding, the dogs a-barking; you shall go on fiddling, and I follow danc-ing Lantæra.

*Wonderful Year*, p. 84: The cuckoo, like a single sole fiddler that reels from tavern to tavern, plied it all the day long; lambs friskt up and down in the valleys, kids and goats leapt to and fro on the mountains: shepherds sat piping, country wenches singing: lovers made sonnets for their lasses, whilst they made garlands for their lovers: and, as the city was frolic, so was the country merry.

*Shoemaker's Holiday* II. 5: Sʏʙɪʟ. The deer came running into the barn through the orchard and over the pale; I wot well I looked as pale as a new cheese to see him. But whip, says Goodman Pin-close, up with his flail, and our Nick with a prong, and down he fell, and they upon him, and I upon them. By my troth, we had such sport; and in the end we ended him; his throat we cut, flayed him, unhorned him, and my lord mayor shall eat of him anon when he comes.

*The Peace is Broken*, p. 103 : But at the last drums were heard to thunder, and trumpets to sound alarums, murmur ran up and down every street, and confusion did beat at the gates of every city, men met together, and ran in herds like deer frighted, or rather like bears chafed, or else seeking for prey.

## Act V, Scene 4.

### (332 solid lines; word-average, .169)

### Mixed passage.

The following passage certainly shows the presence of Dekker, and possibly a touch of Webster's pen in revising :

*Westward Ho* V. 4 : Take my counsel, I 'll ask no fee for 't:

*Appius and Virginia* III. 2 : I only give you my opinion, I ask no fee for 't.

*White Devil* I. 2 : This is my counsel, and I ask no fee for 't.

bar out host, banish mine hostess, beat away the chamberlain, let the ostlers walk, enter you the chambers peaceably, lock the doors gingerly, look upon your wives woefully, but upon the evildoers most wickedly.

*Whore of Babylon*, p. 213 : Your gallants drink here right worshipfully, eat most impudently, dice most swearingly, swear most damnably, quarrel most desperately, and put up most cowardly.

*The Devil is in It*, p. 280 : You are to say grace demurely, wait on the Prior's trencher soberly, steal a mouthful cunningly, and munch it up in a corner hungerly.

Aside from the above, there are no passages from Webster.

## Other passages from Dekker.

(a) *Westward Ho* V. 4 : Tenterhook. A little low woman, sayest thou, in a velvet cap ?
*Honest Whore II* III. 1 : Orlando. A little tiny woman, lower than your ladyship by head and shoulders.

(b) *Westward Ho* V. 4: We are bought and sold in Brainford market.
*Wonder of a Kingdom* IV : My health is bought and sold, sir, then by you. [*]

(c) *Westward Ho* V. 4: Say you should rattle up the constable, thrash all the country together, hedge in the house with flails, pikestaves, and pitchforks, take your wives napping, these western smelts nibbling, etc.
[Compare with last parallel passage of V. 3; also for use of 'nibbling,' see *Westward Ho* II. 2, passage (c)].

(d) *Westward Ho* V. 4: Say ... that, like so many Vulcans, every smith should discover his Venus dancing with Mars in a net.
*Honest Whore I* V. 2 : We see you, old man, for all you dance in a net.

(e) *Westward Ho* V. 4: Ay, but when light wives make heavy husbands, let these husbands play mad Hamlet, and cry, 'Revenge.'
*Seven Deadly Sins* 7 [*Cruelty*]: I would ... that every miserable debtor that so dies might be buried at his creditor's door, that when he strides over him he might think he still rises up, like the ghost in *Jeronimo*, crying 'Revenge.'
*Lanthorn and Candlelight*, p. 262: But if any mad Hamlet, hearing this. [*]

(f) *Westward Ho* V. 4 : An almond, parrot.
*Honest Whore I* V. 2 : Here's an almond for parrot.
*Fortunatus* I. 1 : My tongue speaks no language but an almond for a parrot. [*]

(g) *Westward Ho* V. 4: The collier has a sackful of news to empty.

*Satiro-mastix*, p. 192: Asin. I have a sackful of news for thee; thou shalt plague some of them, if God send us life and health together. Hor. It's no matter, empty thy sack anon.

(h) *Westward Ho* V. 4: 'S foot, you ha' spoiled half already, and you'll spoil all if you dam not up your mouths.
*Roaring Girl* IV. 2: 'S foot, you'll spoil all. [?]

(i) *Westward Ho* V. 4: At hand, sir, with a wet finger. [*]
[See *Westward Ho* II. 2, passage (k)].

(j) *Westward Ho* V. 4: This bawd has been damned five hundred times.
[For use of 'five hundred' in Dekker see *Northward Ho* III. 1, passage (a)].

(k) *Westward Ho* V. 4: For either a cunning woman has a chamber in her house, or a physician, or a picture-maker, or an attorney, because all these are good cloaks for the rain. And then, if the female party that's cliented above-stairs be young, she's a squire's daughter of low degree, that lies there for physic, or comes up to be placed with a countess; if of middle age, she's a widow, and has suits at the term or so.

*Honest Whore I* II. 1: Hip. What may this lady be whom you call coz.? Flu. Faith, sir, a poor gentlewoman, of passing good carriage; one that has some suits in law, and lies here in an attorney's house.

*Lanthorn and Candlelight*, p. 268: And where must her lodging be taken up but in the house of some citizen, whose known reputation she borrows, or rather steals, putting it on as a cloak to cover her deformities. ... As, for example, she will lie in some scrivener's house, and so under the colour of coming to have a bond made, she herself may write *Noverint universi*. And, though the law threaten to hit her never so often, yet hath she subtle defences to ward off the blows. For, if gallants haunt the house, then spreads she these colours: she is a captain or a lieutenant's wife in the Low Countries, and they come with letters from the soldier her husband. If merchants resort to her, then hoists she up these sails, she is wife to the master of a ship, and they bring news that her husband put in at the straits. ... If shopkeepers come to her, with 'what do you lack' in their mouths, then she takes up such and such commodities. ... But if the stream of her fortunes run low, and that none but apronmen launch forth there, then keeps she a politic tempster's [seamstress?] shop, or she starches them.

(l) *Westward Ho* V. 4: And therefore set the hare's-head against the goose-giblets.
*Shoemaker's Holiday* II. 1:

> I'd set mine old debts against my new driblets,
> And the hare's foot against the goose-giblets. [*]

(m) *Westward Ho* V. 4: Look you, your schoolmaster has been in France, and lost his hair. [*Takes off his false hair.*]
*Honest Whore II* II. 3:

> CAND. My man? my master, though his head be bare,
> But he's so courteous, he'll pull off his hair.

LOD. Nay, if your service be so hot a man cannot keep his hair on, I'll serve you no longer. [*Takes off his false hair.*]
BRIDE. Is this your schoolmaster?
*Roaring Girl* IV. 2: GREEN. Nay, gentlemen, seeing your women are so hot, I must lose my hair in their company, I see. [*Takes off his false hair.*]

## Chapter VI.

## THE PARALLEL-PASSAGE TEST.
### *NORTHWARD HO.*

On the whole, I have not been able to find as many parallel passages for *Northward Ho* as for *Westward Ho*. This may be partly due to the fact that I have not been able to make quite such an exhaustive study for the latter comedy under this head; but I think it is also partly due to the play itself. *Northward Ho*, all things considered, is not quite so typical of Dekker's usual vein as *Westward Ho*; also, Webster had a larger part in it, and it is more difficult to get parallel passages from Webster, for reasons already mentioned. Nevertheless, I have found at least two passages for every scene in *Northward Ho*, usually a much larger number; and here again, as in the earlier comedy, the results of this test, although sometimes a trifle meagre, agree almost perfectly with the results of the three-syllable word-test.

### Act I, Scene 1.

(193 solid lines; word-average, .301)

### Passages from Webster.

(a) *Northward Ho* I. 1: GREEN. Not many nights coming to her and being familiar with her,— MAY. Kissing, and so forth? GREEN. Ay, sir. MAY. And talking to her feelingly? ... What, did she talk feelingly to him, too?
*Devil's Law Case* I. 2:

> I have seen this lord many a time and oft
> Set her in's lap, and talk to her of love
> So feelingly.

(b) *Northward Ho* I. 1: I'll deliver it to you, with protestation beforehand, I seek not to publish every gentlewoman's dishonour, only by the passage of my discourse to have you censure the state of our quarrel.

*Cure for a Cuckold* V. 1:

> Yet, misconceive me not, I do entreat you,
> To think I can be of that easy wit
> Or of that malice to defame a lady,
> Were she so kind as to expose herself.

(c) *Northward Ho* I. 1: MAY. And entertained your love? GREEN. As meadows do April.

*White Devil* IV. 2:

> Instruction to thee
> Comes like sweet showers to overhardened ground;
> They wet, but pierce not deep.

*Appius and Vir.* IV. 2:

> Thou lov'st me, Appius, as the earth loves rain;
> Thou fain would'st swallow me.

*Devil's Law Case* I. 2:

> If crying had been regarded, maidenheads
> Had ne'er been lost; at least some appearance.
> Of crying as an April shower i' the sunshine. [?]

(d) *Northward Ho* I. 1: The violence, as it seemed, of her affection—but, alas, it proved her dissembling—would, at my coming and departing, bedew her eyes with love-drops: O, she could the art of woman most feelingly!

*White Devil* V. 3:

> Had women navigable rivers in their eyes,
> They would dispend them all: surely, I wonder
> Why we should wish more rivers to the city,
> When they sell water so good cheap. I tell thee,
> These are but moonish shades of griefs or fears;
> There's nothing sooner dry than women's tears.

[Compare also use of ' feelingly ' in passage (b)].

(e) *Northward Ho* I. 1: In the passage of our loves, amongst other favours of greater value, she bestowed upon me this ring, which, she protested, was her husband's gift.

*Cure for a Cuckold* V. 1:

Roch.                          Yet, to satisfy you,
    And in some kind, too, to delight myself,
    Those bracelets and the carcanet she wears
    She gave me once.
Less. They were the first and special tokens passed
    Betwixt her and her husbaud.

(f) *Northward Ho* I. 1: Lying with her, as I say, and rising somewhat early from her in the morning.

*Duchess of Malfi* III. 2:

    Wherefore, still, when you lie with my lady,
    Do you rise so early?

### Passages from Dekker.

(a) *Northward Ho* I. 1: True, but yet it comes scant of the prophecy,—Lincoln was, London is, and York shall be.

*Wonderful Year*, p. 101: Now and never till now did she laugh to scorn that worm-eaten proverb of Lincoln was, London is, and York shall be. [*]

(b) *Northward Ho* I. 1: Bellamont. Come, strive to blow over these clouds. Mayberry. Not a cloud; you shall have clean moonshine.

*Whore of Babylon*, p. 265:

    All these black clouds we clear: look up, 't is day,
    The sun shines on thee still.

It will be noticed that one of the two parallel passages from Dekker in this scene is from the speeches of Mayberry; that he has very little part in the parallel passages from Webster; and that the other parallel from Dekker is in the dialogue with the chamberlain. This is interesting in the light of the word-test for this scene.

### Northward Ho I. 1.

| | Solid lines. | Words. | Average. |
|---|---|---|---|
| Greenshield | 62 | 28 | .452 |
| Featherstone | 12 | 5 | .417 |
| Chamberlain | 13 | 0 | .000 |
| Mayberry | 54 | 7 | .130 |
| Bellamont | 52 | 18 | .346 |
| Totals | 193 | 58 | .301 |

*Conclusion.* When we remember how much more the same number of passages count from Webster than from Dekker, we see at a glance that the parallel-passage test favors Webster decidedly in this scene.

### Act I, Scene 2.
### (108 solid lines; word-average, .185)
### No passages from Webster.
### Passages from Dekker.

(a) *Northward Ho* I. 2: Drawer, tie my shoe, prithee.
*Shoemaker's Holiday* III. 4: Hans, pray thee, tie my shoe.

(b) *Northward Ho* 1. 2: And is every one that swims in a taffeta gown lettuce for your lips.
*Westward Ho* II. 2: For as the cobbler in the night-time walks with his lantern, the merchant and the lawyer with his link, and the courtier with his torch, so every lip has his lettuce to himself.

(c) *Northward Ho* I. 2: I'm as melancholy now as Fleet-street in a long vacation.
*Satiro-mastix*, p. 186: What senseless thing in all the house that is not now as melancholy as a new set-up schoolmaster? [*]

(d) *Northward Ho* I. 2: Those poor wenches that before Christmas fled westward with bag and baggage.

*The Peace is Broken*, p. 122: A great crew of her followers, that were not able with bag and baggage to march after her in that progress. ... p. 140: Whereupon many thousands with bag and baggage were compelled to leave the city and cling only to the suburbs.

*Gull's Hornbook*, chap. 8: When the siege breaks up, and at your marching away with bag and baggage. [*]

(e) *Northward Ho* I. 2: No matter though it be a tavern that has blown up his master; it shall be in trade still.

*The Peace is Broken*, p. 96: Playhouses stand, like taverns that have cast out their masters, the doors locked up.

(f) *Northward Ho* I. 2: It shall then be given out that I'm a gentlewoman of such a birth, such a wealth, have had such a breeding, and so forth, and of such a carriage and such qualities, and so forth.

*Lanthorn and Candlelight*, p. 252: They fall in study with the general rule of their knavery; and those are, first, to give out that their master is a gentleman of such and such means, in such a shire ... that he is come to receive so many hundred pounds upon land that he hath sold.

(g) *Northward Ho* I. 2: LEVER. If thou 't have a lodging westward, Doll, I 'll fit thee. DOLL. At Tyburn, will you not?

*Roaring Girl* II. 1: LAXTON. Prithee, sweet, plump Moll, when shalt thou and I go out a' town together? MOLL. Whither? to Tyburn, prithee?

[Notice that there is the same quibble on going to Tyburn in both].

### Act I, Scene 3.

(181 solid lines; word-average, .100)

No passages from Webster.[1]

Passages from Dekker.

(a) *Northward Ho* I. 3: Up, sir, down, sir! so, sir.—

*Honest Whore II* V. 2: My twenty pounds did fly high,

---

[1] Two passages from Webster having a slight likeness are given in the foot-notes further on; but in each case there are two or three closer parallels from Dekker.

sir, your wife's gown did fly low, sir; whither fly you now, sir?

(b) *Northward Ho* I. 3: BELLAMONT. He does not look like a bawd; he has no double chin. PRENTICE. No, sir, nor my breath does not stink, I smell not of garlic or *aqua-vitæ*.

*The Peace is Broken*, p. 122: A company of double-chinned, poltfooted, stinking-breathed bawds, who with pewter bottles of *aqua-vitæ* at their girdles,—etc.

(c) *Northward Ho* I. 3: Never sold one maidenhead ten several times, first to an Englishman, then to a Welshman, then to a Dutchman, then to a pocky Frenchman.

[The list of nationalities here is an almost sure mark of Dekker. Compare passages in *Westward Ho* II. 1 (r)].

(d) *Northward Ho* I. 3: Never had the grincomes.

*Whore of Babylon*, p. 242. Then she has got the pox, and lying at my host Grincomes. [?]

[The word *grincomes*, meaning the venereal disease, may have been common colloquially; but it is not common with the dramatists nor found—as far as I can discover—in Webster].

(e) *Northward Ho* I. 3: MAY. When two virginal jacks skip up, as the key of my instrument goes down. BELL. They are two wicked elders.

*Satiro-mastix*, p. 218: Hark, hither, Susanna, beware of these two wicked elders.

*Satiro-mastix*, p. 187; When we have husbands, we play upon them like virginal jacks; they must rise and fall to our humours.[1]

(f) *Northward Ho* I. 3: Inquire at one of mine aunts.[2]

*Shoemaker's Holiday* IV. 2: Your cousin? No, master; one of your aunts. [*]

(g) *Northward Ho* I. 3: Here's the party, sir.

[1] This last quibble was of course common.
[2] *Aunt* was a common cant term for bawd, but expressions like the above are favorites with Dekker. Others might have been collected.

*Wonder of a Kingdom* IV : Gentili. What next? Servant.
The party, sir.  [?]

(h) *Northward Ho* I. 8 :

> If ever I had thought unclean,
> In detestation of your nuptial pillow,
> Let sulphur drop from heaven, and nail my body
> Dead to this earth.

*Whore of Babylon*, p. 194 :

> Can yonder roof, that's nailed so fast with stars,
> Cover a head so impious and not crack ?
> That sulphur, boiling o'er celestial fires,
> May drop in whizzing flakes with scalding vengeance
> On such a horrid sin !

p. 272 :

> This stratagem dropt down from heaven in fire.

p. 210 :

> And to forge three-forked thunderbolts at home,
> Whilst I melt sulphur here.

p. 277 :

> Fall thunder,
> And wedge me into earth, stiff as I am.

(i) *Northward Ho* I. 3 :

> That slave, that damnéd Fury,
> Whose whips are in your tongue to torture me,
> Casting an eye unlawful on my cheek,
> Haunted your threshold daily.

*Wonder of a Kingdom* III :

> If you spy any man that has a look
> Stigmatically drawn, like to a Fury's,
> Able to fright, to such I'll give large pay,
> To watch and ward for poor snakes night and day,
> And whip 'em soundly if they approach my gates.

*Sun's Darling* III :

> Whence come these thunderbolts, what furies haunt you ?

(j) *Northward Ho* I. 3:

> And threw forth
> All tempting baits which lust and credulous youth
> Apply to our frail sex.

*Honest Whore I* II. 1:

> And then a fourth
> Should have this golden hook and lascivious bait
> Thrown out to the full length.

*Wonder of a Kingdom* I:

> Bait a hook with gold and with it ...

(k) *Northward Ho* I. 3:

> Lodge me in some discomfortable vault,
> Where neither sun nor moon may touch my sight.[1]

*Fortunatus* V. 1:

> Lock me in some cave,
> Where staring wonder's eye shall not be guilty
> To my abhorrèd looks.

*Whore of Babylon*, p. 232:

> Or like to ancresses
> Close up yourselves in artificial walls.

(l) *Northward Ho* I. 3:

> I take your word you 're honest; which good men,
> Very good men will scarce do to their wives.

*Wonder of a Kingdom* IV: ALPHONSINA. I 'll do that, then, which some citizens will not do to some lord[s]. NICOLETTI. What's that? ALPHONSINA. Take your word; I come.

(m) *Northward Ho* I. 3:

> I 'll candy o'er my words and sleek my brow.

---

[1] The following passage from Webster also bears some resemblance, but it is obviously weaker than the two passages from Dekker combined:

*Duchess of Malfi* III. 2:

> I would have thee build
> Such a room for him as our anchorites
> To holier use inhabit. Let not the sun
> Shine on him till he 's dead.

*Wonder of a Kingdom* IV:

> Thou hast candied
> Thy sweet but poisonous language, to dishonour
> Me, thy most wretched sister.

*Satiro-mastix*, p. 220: I 'll give thee none but sugar-candy words, I will not, Puss.

(n) *Northward Ho* I. 3:

> I will bring home these serpents and allow them
> The heat of mine own bosom.

*Whore of Babylon*, p. 249:

> A snake that in my bosom once I warmed.

*The Devil is in It*, p. 342:

> This is the snake whose sting,
> Being kept warm in the bosom of a king,
> Struck him to th' heart.

*Match Me in London* IV:

> Were the beds
> Of twenty thousand snakes laid in this bosom.
> . . . I have warmed a snake in my bosom.

*Honest Whore II* I. 2:

> Her bosom
> Gives warmth to no such snakes.  [*]

(o) *Northward Ho* I. 3:

> I 'll fetch my blow
> Fair and afar off, and as fencers use,
> Though at the foot I strike, the head I 'll bruise.[1]

*Whore of Babylon*, p. 198:

> This were with fencers basely to give ground
> When the first bout may speed.

---

[1] The following passage from Webster should also be given here; but, though similar in thought, it has no such little touches of phraseology as the ones from Dekker:

*White Devil* II. 4:

> Alas, the poorest of their forced dislikes
> At a limb proffers, but at heart it strikes.

p. 238:

Your ward blows off from her, that at all weapons
Strikes at your head.

*The Peace is Broken*, p. 124: The blows that foreign
enemies give are broken for the most part, because the
weapon is always seen and put by; otherwise they would
cut deep and draw blood, where, by such prevention, they
scarce give bruises.

(p) *Northward Ho* I. 3: BELLAMONT. From whence come
you, pray? PHILIP. From the house of prayer and fasting,
the Counter. BELLAMONT. Art thou not ashamed to be seen
to come out of a prison? PHILIP. No, God's my judge;
but I was ashamed to go into prison.

*Whore of Babylon*, p. 212: TITANIA. Now, sirrah, where
have you been? PLAIN DEALING. Where have I been? I have
been in the bravest prison. TITANIA. What prison? a brave
prison? Can there be a brave prison?

(q) *Northward Ho* I. 3: I confess I took up a petticoat
and a raised forepart for her: but who has to do with that?

*Sun's Darling* III: RAY. Brave ladies have their humors.
FOLLY. Who has to do with that but brave lords?

*Honest Whore I* III. 1: I am, sir; what hast thou to do
with that?

(r) *Northward Ho* I. 3: Her name is Dorothy, sir; I hope
that's no ill name.

*Honest Whore II* V. 2: I'm not ashamed of my name,
sir; my name is Mistress Doll Target, a Western gentlewoman.

(s) *Northward Ho* I. 3: The northern man loves white
meats, the southery man sallads, the Essex man a calf, the
Kentish man a wag-tail, the Lancashire man an egg-pie, the
Welshman leeks and cheese, and your Londoners raw mutton.

*Westward Ho* II. 2:[1] The lob has his lass, the collier his
dowdy, the western man his pug, the serving man his punk,

---

[1] *Westward Ho* II. 2, is so obviously Dekker's that we can,
I think, use it to prove other scenes.

the student his nun in White-friars, the Puritan his sister, and
the lord his lady,

(t) *Northward Ho* I. 3. Farewell, Father Snot.
*Honest Whore I* II. 1 : 'Tis the dreamingest snotty nose. [?]

## Act II, Scene 1.
### (284 solid lines ; word-average, .078)
### No passages from Webster.
### Passages from Dekker.

(a) *Northward Ho* II. 1 : If we have but good draughts
in my peterboat, fresh salmon, you sweet villains, shall be
no meat with us.[1]
*Honest Whore I* II. 1 : So, give the fresh salmon line now ;
let him come ashore.
*Honest Whore II* III. 2 : Hast angled ? hast cut up this
fresh salmon ?
*Honest Whore II* V. 2 : But the poor salmon-trout is now
in the net.

(b) *Northward Ho* II. 1 : HORNET. How does my chain show,
now I walk ? DOLL. If thou wert hung in chains, thou
couldst not show better.
*The Devil is in It*, p. 358 : My chain, let me hang in
chains, so it be my gold chain.

(c) *Northward No* II. 1 : A Dutch merchant that would
spend all that he's able to make i' the Low-Countries but
to take measure of my Holland sheets when I lie in 'em.
*Westward Ho* II. 2 : If your husband has given up his
cloak, let another take measure of you in his jerkin. [*]

(d) *Northward Ho* II. 1 : O, I shall burst if I cut not my
lace, I am so vexed.
*Honest Whore I* II. 1 : Fie fie, cut my lace, good servant ;

[1] Compare with *Northward Ho* IV. 3, (a).

I shall have the mother presently, I'm so vexed at this horse-plumb.

(e) *Northward Ho* II. 1: ALLUM. When is it to be paid? DOLL. Between one and two.

*Roaring Girl* IV. 1: MOLL. What's o' clock here? [*Aside by Sir Alexander*]. MOLL. Between one and two.

*The Devil is in It*, p. 296:

> This day 'twixt one and two a gallant 's bound
> To pay 400 crowns to free his lands.

(f) *Northward Ho* II. 1: By this iron, which is none of God's angel.

*Satiro-mastix*, p. 193: I markt, by this candle, which is none of God's angels.[1]

(g) *Northward Ho* II. 1: O, there is the most abominable[2] seer.

*Satiro-mastix*, p. 214: SIR VAUGHAN. As good seer as would make any hungry man . . . eat and he had any stomach.

(h) *Northward Ho* II. 1: I'll run headlongs by and by, and batter away money for a new coach to jolt you in. . . . I will buy not only a coach with four wheels, but also a white mare and a stone horse too, because they shall traw you very lustily

*Patient Grissil* III. 2: And her shall buy her new card to ride in,[3] and two new fine horses, and more blue coats and padges to follow her heels.

*Roaring Girl* II. 1: [Laxton to Moll] I'll hire a coach with four horses.

(i) *Northward Ho* II. 1: He paid that shot, and then shot pistolets into my pockets.

*Match Me in London* III:

> In thy bosom, for thy pistolets,
> I'll give thee pistols; in a piece might have been mine
> Thou shoot'st or mean'st to shoot, but I'll change thine.

---

[1] Pointed out by Dyce.

[2] Dyce says that 'abominable' here means 'good'.

[3] Suggested by Stoll.

Act II, Scene 2.

(201 solid lines; word-average, .313)

Passages from Webster.

(a) *Northward Ho* II. 2: Bid them extremely welcome,
though thou wish their throats cut; 'tis in fashion.
*Duchess of Malfi* I. 1:

> As I have seen some
> Feed in a lord's dish, half a sleep, not seeming
> To listen to any talk; and yet these rogues
> Have cut his throat in a dream.

*Duchess of Malfi* I. 1: Whose throat must I cut?

(b) *Northward Ho* II. 2: I was in doubt I should have
grown fat of late: an it were not for law-suits and fear of
our wives, we rich men should grow out of all compass.
*Duchess of Malfi* III. 1:

> You have not been in law, friend Delio,
> Nor in prison, nor a suitor at the court,
> Nor begg'd the reversion of some great man's place,
> Nor troubled with an old wife, which doth make
> Your time so insensibly hasten.

II. 1: Your arm, Cariola, do I not grow fat?

(c) *Northward Ho* II. 2: Look, my wife's colour rises
already.
*Duchess of Malfi* II. 1: Good, her colour rises. [?]

(d) *Northward Ho* II. 2: God refuse me, they are lying
rascals.
*White Devil* I. 2: God refuse me, Might I advise you now.[1]
*Appius and Virginia* II. 2: Refuse me, if such traitorous
rogues. [*]

(e) *Northward Ho* II. 2: Wise men should deal by their
wives as the sale of ordnance passeth in England: . . . if
she hold pure metal two years and fly to several pieces in
the third, repair the ruins of her honesty at your charges.

---

[1] A common oath, but apparently a favorite with Webster, and
not with Dekker.

*Duchess of Malfi* III. 5:

> O misery, like to a rusty o'er-charged cannon,
> Shall I never fly in pieces.

## Doubtful passage.

*Northward Ho* II. 2: Oh God, that I might have my will of him! an it were not for my husband, I'd scratch out his eyes presently.

*White Devil* II. 1:

> To dig the strumpet's eyes out; let her lie
> Some twenty months a-dying!

*Patient Grissil* V. 2: An I were Grissil, I would pull her eyes out. [?]

## Passage from Dekker.

*Northward Ho* II. 2: Your citizens' wives are like partridges, the hens are better than the cocks.

*Honest Whore II* I. 3: The hen shall not overcrow the cock; I'll sharpen your spurs.

[See also *Westward Ho* V. 4.]

*Conclusion.* The evidence is weak for both authors, but certainly favors Webster as far as it goes. The very absence of good parallels from Dekker seems significant, when we compare this scene with those certainly written by him.

## Act III, Scene 1.

### (127 solid lines; word-average, .276)

### Passages from Webster.

(a) *Northward Ho* III. 1: DOLL. I will bestow them, indeed, upon a Welsh captain, one that loves cheese better than venison; for if you should but get three or four Cheshire cheeses, and set them a-running down Highgate-

hill, he would make more haste after them than after the
best kennel of hounds in England.  What think you of my
device?  BELLAMONT.  'Fore God, a very strange device and
a cunning one.

*Devil's Law Case* V. 4:

There was a strange experiment of a fencer ...
The Welshman in his play, do what the fencer could,
Hung still an arse; he could not for his life
Make him come on bravely; till one night at supper,
Observing what a deal of Parma-cheese
His scholar devour'd, goes ingeniously
The next morning and makes a spacious button
For his foil of toasted cheese; and as sure as you live,
That made him come on the braveliest.

(b) *Northward Ho* III. 1: I think thou art a most admirable, brave, beautiful whore.

*White Devil* IV. 1:

God's precious! you shall be a brave, great lady,
A stately and advanced whore.  [?]

## Passages from Dekker.

(a) *Northward Ho* III. 1: Thou shalt see me make a fool
of a poet, that hath made five hundred fools.

*Honest Whore I* II. 1: BELLAFRONT.  How many gentlemen
hast thou served thus? ROGER.  None but five hundred, besides prentices and serving-men.

*Honest Whore II* V. 2: And that's more than fifteen women
among five hundred dare swear.

*Lanthorn and Candlelight*, p 245: This fetches money from
him, and this cozens five hundred beside.

*Honest Whore II* III. 2: MAT.  Knowest thou never a damned broker about the city? ORL.  Damned broker? yes,
five hundred.

(b) *Northward Ho* III. 1: Sometimes be merry and stand
upon thy pantofles.

*Raven's Almanac*, p. 198: Now did Signieur Cobbler stand
no more on his pantofles.

(c) *Northward Ho* III. 1: I'll have you make twelve posies for a dozen of cheese trenchers.

*Honest Whore I* V. 1: And as one of our cheese trenchers says very[1] learnedly,—['posy' follows.]

[d] *Northward Ho* III. 1: I had three nest of them [goblets] given me by a nobleman.

*Wonderful Year*, p. 91:

> And now do chirrup by fine golden nests
> Of well-hatcht bowls, such as do breed in feasts.

*Honest Whore II* I. 3: Didst e'er see such a nest of caps?

The thing to be noticed in the above is the use of the word 'nest' in the sense of several together or a set. This word is used by other dramatists,[2] but it is very rare; and the fact that Dekker uses it twice elsewhere would imply that he was the man who used it in *Northward Ho*.

*Conclusion.* The passages from both authors are few in number and poor in quality; they seem to imply that both men had some share in this scene, and that is about all.

## Act III, Scene 2.

### (142 solid lines; word-average, .183)

### No passages from Webster.

### Passages from Dekker.

(a) *Northward Ho* III. 2: Whilst I go and take but two kisses, but two kisses from sweet Featherstone.

*Match Me in London* V:

> That whilst his wild lust wanders, I may fly
> To my sweet husband's arms.

---

[1] Pointed out by Dyce.

[2] Dyce gives one instance each from Marston and Armin. It is also found once in Rowley.

(b) *Northward Ho* III. 2:
O, I am sick, I am sick, I am
sick. ...

GREEN. How does she, Master Featherstone?

FEATHER. Very ill, sir, she's
troubled with the mother extremely: I held down her
belly even now, and I might
feel it rise. ...

GREEN. I will find a remedy
for this walking, if all the doctors in town can sell it.

*Wonder of a Kingdom* II:
O, my sweet lord, she 's at it
again, at it again ...

FLORENCE. How now, nurse,
how does my Fiametta? ...

NURSE. It takes her all
over with a pricking; first
about her stomach, and then
she heaves and heaves, that
no man with all his weight,
can keep her down. ...

FLORENCE. I will give half
my dukedom for her health.

(c) *Northward Ho* III. 2: Pretty little rogue! I 'll wake
her and make her ashamed of it.

*Satiro-mastix*, p. 211: Ah, little rogue, your wit has picked
up her crumbs pretty and well. [?]

(d) *Northward Ho* III. 2: KATE. An I were where I would
be, in your bed,—pray, pardon me, was 't you, Master
Featherstone?—hem, I should be well then. SQUIRREL.
[aside to Leapfrog.] Mark how she wrings him by the fingers.
KATE. Good night.

*Lanthorn and Candlelight*, p. 301: Lust with Prodigality
were heard to stand closely kissing; and, wringing one
another by the hand, softly to whisper out four or five
good nights.

## Act IV, Scene 1.

(287 solid lines; word-average, .223)

No passages from Webster.

Passages from Dekker.

(a) *Northward Ho* IV. 1: CAP. JEN. You are a poet, sir,
are you? BELL. I'm haunted with a fury, sir.

*Satiro-mastix*, p. 240: My delicate, poetical fury, th'ast hit
it to a hair.

*Sun's Darling* III:
Whence come these thunderbolts, what furies haunt you?

(b) *Northward Ho* IV. 1: Ow, by gad, out o' cry.
*Shoemaker's Holiday* II. 1: O yes, out of cry, by my troth.
*Patient Grissil* II. 1: Sir Owen is clad out a' cry.[1]
—Sir Emulo is friends out a' cry now.[1]
—By God, is out a' cry friends.[1]

(c) *Northward Ho* IV. 1: Cap. Jenkins. But are you sure Duke Pepper-noon will give you such good urds behind your back to your face?[1]
*Satiro-mastix*, p. 236: By Sesu, 'tis best you give good urds, too.[2]

(d) *Northward Ho* IV. 1: God udge me, all France may hap die in your debt for this.
*Patient Grissil* III. 2: As God udge me,[1] &c.
—God udge me, not love her cousin.
—God udge me, her shall not.

(e) *Northward Ho* IV. 1: There was one young Styanax of Monmouthshire, was a madder Greek as any is in all England.
[See *Westward Ho* II. 1, passage (k).]

(f) *Northward Ho* IV. 1:    *Satiro-mastix*, pp. 192–194:[3]
I'll borrow your judgment:    Damn me, if it be not the
look you, sir, I'm writing    best that ever came from me,
a tragedy, the tragedy of    if I have any judgment; look,
*Young Astyanax.* ...       sir, 'tis an *Epithalamium* for
                       Sir Walter Terrel's wedding. ...
Bellamont. O, ay, ay, ay,    Horace. Yet with kisses
man; he's the only courtier   will they fee thee, my muse
that I know there. But what   hath marched (dear rogue)

[1] Suggested by Bangs.
[2] This may seem like a matter of dialect rather than authorship; but the Welshman Randall in Rowley's *Match at Midnight* says 'good words,' not 'good urds.'
[3] The passages from both plays are not all given in their order, but those from *Satiro-mastix* are all between p. 192 and p. 194.

do you think that I may come to by this? . . .

no farther yet; but how is 't? how is 't? nay, prithee, good Asinius, deal plainly. . . .

An acrostic were good upon her name, methinks. . . .

You have seen my acrostics? . . .

O, sir, 'tis a figure in poetry: mark how 'tis followed: 'Rode on their own roofs,' &c. . . .

Mark now, dear Asinius: 'Let these virgins quickly see thee,' &c. . . .

A gentlewoman that I am fallen in withal, over head and ears in affections and natural desires. . , .

Over head and ears, i' faith. . . .

Could the little horse that ambled on the top of Paul's carry all the people.

I have heard a' the horses walking a' the top of Paul's.

(g) *Northward Ho* IV. 1:

> Now the wild people, greedy of their griefs,
> Longing to see that which their thoughts abhorred,
> Prevented day and rode on their own roofs, . . .
> Making all neighbouring houses tiled with men.

*King's Entertainment*, p. 227: The day for whose sake these wonders of wood climbed thus up into the clouds, is now come; being so early up by reason of artificial lights, which wakened it, that the sun overslept himself, and rose not in many hours after, yet bringing with it into the very bosom of the city a world of people. The streets seemed to be paved with men; stalls instead of rich wares were set up with children, open casements filled up with women.

(h) *Northward Ho* IV. 1: BELL. An acrostic were good upon her name, methinks. CAP. JENKINS. Cross sticks! I would not be too cross, master poet.

*Satiro-mastix*, p. 241: SIR VAUGHAN. For he shall make another thalimium, or cross-sticks, or some polinodies with a few nappy-grams in them.

(i) *Northward Ho* IV. 1: Captain, what would you press

me for? ... Is she i' faith—captain, be honest and tell true
—is she honest? ... Look you, captain, I 'll show you why
I ask. ... Shall she come in, captain? ... Captain, lie you
in ambush behind the hangings.

*Satiro-mastix*, pp. 199–201: O, our honest captain, come,
prithee, let us see ... By Jesu, within this hour, save you,
captain Tucca. ... Yes, captain, this is my poor lodging. ...
Morrow, captain Tucca, will you whiff this morning? ...
To do you pleasure, captain, I will. Dear captain, but one
word ... Captain Tucca, but half a word in your ear ...
Captain, I know upon what even bases I stand. ... For our
sake, captain, nay, prithee hold. ... With all my heart,
captain Tucca. ... Never, captain, I thank God.

(j) *Northward Ho* IV. 1: This goat's pizzle of thine.
*Satiro-mastix*, p. 200: Art thou there, goat's pizzle.[1]
*Honest Whore II* IV. 2: Gray-beard, goat's pizzle.

(k) *Northward Ho* IV. 1: Garlic has a white head and
a green stalk; then why should not I?
*Honest Whore II* I. 2: Though my head be like a leek,
white, may not my heart be like the blade, green?[1]
*Lanthorn and Candlelight*, p. 297: Or that others should
laugh at them to see white heads growing upon green
stalks. [*]

(l) *Northward Ho* IV 1: Did I not tell you, old man,
that she'd win any game when she came to bearing?
*Roaring Girl* IV. 2: O, the trial is when she comes to
bearing.

(m) *Northward Ho* IV. 1: And, as if I were a bawd, no
ring pleases me but a Death's-head.
*The Peace is Broken*, p. 122: Bawds, who with pewter
bottles of *aqua-vitæ* at their girdles, rings with Death's-heads
on their forefingers, &c.
*Match Me in London* V: Thy wife, for the hoop-ring thou
marriedst her withal, hath sworn to send thee a Death's-head.

[1] The first of these parallels was pointed out by Stoll. An
expression more or less like (k) seems to have been proverbial,
and is traced back by Dyce through Chaucer to Boccaccio.

(n) *Northward Ho* IV. 1 : CAP. JENKINS. I sharge you in Apollo's name, whom you belong to, see her forthcoming.

*Satiro-mastix*, p. 257 : In God's name and the king's I sharge you to ring it out from all our ears. [?]

(o) *Northward Ho* IV. 1 : CAP. JENKINS. You, Mistress Salamanders, that fear no burning.

*Satiro-mastix*, p. 215 : SIR VAUGHN. I will quench the flame out of your name, and you shall be christened Peter Salamander.

*Satiro-mastix*, p. 241 : Right, Peter is'my salamander; what of him? But Peter is never burnt.

(p) *Northward Ho* IV. 1 : CAP. JENKINS. Does the poet play Torkin and cast my Lucresie's water too in huggermugger.

*Satiro-mastix*, p. 214 : One word, Sir Quintilian, in huggermugger. [*]

(q) *Northward Ho* IV. 1 : Would I low after thee that art a common calf-bearer?

*Sun's Darling* III : HUMOR. When will you sing my praises thus? RAYBRIGHT. Thy praises, that art a common creature. [?]

(r) *Northward Ho* IV. 1 : Greenshield . . . entreats his friend to ride before his wife and fetch the money, because, taking bitter pills, he should prove but a loose fellow if he went, and so durst not go.

*The Devil is in It*, p. 228 :

BRISCO. The physic of your proclamation works:
       Your gilded pills (rolled up in promises
       Of princely favors to his wit, who highest
       Can raise your pleasures) slip so smoothly down
       Your subjects' throats, that all upon a sudden
       Are loosely given.
KING. How loosely given? why count?

## Act IV, Scene 2.
(39 solid lines; word-average, .179)
### No passages from Webster.
### Passages from Dekker.

(a) *Northward Ho* IV. 2: Your Norfolk tumblers are but zanies to cony-catching punks.

*Raven's Almanac*, p. 173: I find likewise that a number of you will fall into certain toils which shall be pitched day and night for you by certain greedy hunters, called punks. ... Yet are they of the nature of dogs, and more nimble than Norfolk tumblers.

(b) *Northward Ho* IV. 2: I think she has sent the poor fellow to Gelder-land.

*Shoemaker's Hol.* II. 3:

Der was een bore van Gelderland,
Frolick sie byen.

*Honest Whore II* V. 2:

I ha' been tried, sir, too, in Gelderland.

## Act IV, Scene 3.
(178 solid lines; word-average, 107)
### No passages from Webster.
### Passages from Dekker.

(a) *Northward Ho* IV. 3: Foh! they as soon as they come to their lands, get up to London, and, like squibs that run upon lines, they keep a spitting of fire and cracking till they have spent all; and when my squib is out, what says his punk? Foh, he stinks.

[This passage, as Mr. Stoll says, is probably imitated from the following passage in Marston's *Fawn*; bnt the extracts from Dekker's later plays given below seem to show that it was Dekker, and not Webster, who imitated Marston.]

*Marston's Fawn*: PAGE. There be squibs, sir, which squibs running upon lines, like some of our gaudy gallants, sir, keep a smother, sir, with flishing and flashing, and in the end, sir, they do, sir—

NYMPHADORA. What, sir? PAGE. Stink, sir.

Dekker's *Whore of Babylon*, p. 230:

> Let us behold these fireworks, that must run
> Upon short lines of life.

*Roaring Girl* V. 1: Used that rogue like a firework to run upon a line betwixt him and me.

*Honest Whore II* II. 1: The fire-works that ran upon lines against my old master, your father, were but to try how my young master, your husband, loved such squibs.

(b) *Northward Ho* IV. 3: What, will these young gentlemen too help us to catch this fresh salmon?

*Honest Whore I* II. 1: So, give the fresh salmon line now; let him come ashore.

*Honest Whore II* III. 2: Hast angled? hast cut up this fresh salmon?

*Roaring Girl* IV. 2: And thou shalt take thy husband casting out his net to catch fresh salmon at Brainford.

(c) *Northward Ho* IV. 3: The prentices made a riot upon my glass windows, the Shrove Tuesday following.

*7 Deadly Sins [6—Shaving]*: They presently (like prentices upon Shrove Tuesday) take the law into their own hands and do as they list. [*]

(d) *Northward Ho* IV. 3:

> I sold her maidenhead once, and I sold her
>                         maidenhead twice,
> And I sold it last to an alderman of York,
> And then I had sold it thrice.

*Northward Ho* I. 3: Never sold one maidenhead ten several times, first to an Englishman, then to a Welshman, then to a Dutchman, then to a pocky Frenchman.

[Dekker's, as shown by list of nationalities. See *Westward Ho* II. 1 for parallels.]

(e) *Northward Ho* IV. 3: Marry muff, sing thou better.

*Satiro-mastix*, p. 202: Marry muff, my man a ginger-bread.

*Honest Whore I* II. 1: Marry muff, a' your counts. [*]

## Act V, Part A.

(384 solid lines; word-average, .341)

Passages from Webster.

(a) *Northward Ho* V. A: Observe him, he's not one of your fat city chuffs. ...

Whose reward is not the rate of a captain newly come out of the Low Countries. ... some angel.

*Devil's Law Case* II. 1: You have certain rich city chuffs.

*White Devil* II. 4:
What hast got,
But, like the weath of captains, a poor handful?

(b) *Northward Ho* V. A: God refuse me, gentlemen. [*]
[See *Northward Ho* II. 2.]

(c) *Northward Ho* V. A: O my unfortunate parents, would you had buried me quick, when you linked me to this misery.

*White Devil* II. 1:

Thou hast a wife, our sister: would I had given
Both her white hands to death, bound and locked fast
In her last winding-sheet, when I gave thee
But one! [?]

(d) Compare the following, chiefly, for general style:

*Northward Ho* V. A: Hostess. An you had sent for me up, and kissed me, and used me like a hostess, 'twould never have grieved me; but to do it to a stranger!

*Devil's Law Case* IV. 2: And once, in truth, he would have had some dealing with me,—which I took; he thought 'twould be the only way in the world to make me keep counsel the better.

I. 2: Win. Very well, sir. You may use me at your pleasure.

Romelio. By no means, Winifred; that were the way
To make thee travel again. ...

WIN. Plague of these unsanctified matches!
                they make us loathe
The most natural desire our grandam
                Eve ever left us.
Force one to marry against their will!
                why, 'tis
A more ungodly work than enclosing
                the commons.

(e) *Northward Ho* V. A: That I might be presently turned into a matter more solid than horn,—into marble.

*White Devil* III. 2: What, are you turned all marble?

(f) *Northward Ho* V. A: Wilt thou hang at my purse, Kate, like a pair of Barbary buttons, to open when 'tis full and close when 'tis empty?

*Duchess of Malfi* II. 2: Tell them that the Devil takes delight to hang at a woman's girdle, like a false rusty watch, that she cannot discern how the time passes.

## Passages from Dekker.

(a) *Northward Ho* V. A: And so all his artillery should have recoiled into his own bosom.

*Match Me in London* III: JOHN. Shoot off the piece you have charged. VALASCO. No, it recoils.

*Wonder of a Kingdom* II: As for my old huckster's artillery, I have walls of chastity strong enough, shoot he never so hard. [?]

(b) *Northward Ho* V. A: And so, after, master citizen sleeps as quietly as if he lay in his own Low Country of Holland, his own linen, I mean, sir.

*Roaring Girl* II. 1: Have I found out one of your haunts? I send you for Hollands, and you 're in the Low Countries with a mischief.

(c) *Northward Ho* V. A: I think when he comes home, poor snail, he 'll not dare to peep forth of doors lest his horns usher him.

*The Peace is Broken*, p. 110: No, but like snails pulling in the horns of their fury, they hid their heads for a time.

*Lanthorn and Candlelight,* p. 254: They are not idle neither; but like snails they venture abroad.

p. 268: If before she swaggered in taverns, now with the snail she stirreth not out of doors.

*Honest Whore II* III. 3: I am a snail, sir, seldom leave my house.

*Lanthorn and Candlelight,* p. 297: Then came forth certain infamous, earthy-minded creatures in the shape of snails, who all the daytime hiding their heads in their shells, lest boys should with two fingers point at them for living basely upon the prostitution of their wives, cared not now before candlelight to shoot out their largest and longest horns.

(d) *Northward Ho* V. A: Have I lost the pleasure of mine eyes, the sweets of my youth, the wishes of my blood, and the portion of my friends, to be thus dishonored, to be reputed vile in London, whilst my husband prepares common diseases for me at Ware?

*Roaring Girl* IV. 2:

> Did I for this lose all my friends, refuse
> Rich hopes and golden fortunes, to be made
> A stale to a common whore?

(e) *Northward Ho* V. A: Look you, sir, you gallants visit citizens' houses, as the Spaniard first sailed to the Indies.

*The Devil is in It,* p. 266:

> That men to find Hell, now, new ways have sought,
> As Spaniards did to the Indies.

*Conclusion.* When we remember that this is by far the longest scene in the two plays—having a total of 384 solid lines—we see that five passages from Dekker, although four of them are fairly close, do not forbid giving most of this scene to Webster. It must be confessed, however, that most of the parallels from Webster in this scene are weak. In considering this, we must bear in mind, as was said before, the small range of his extant writing, and the fact that it is nearly all of a different kind.

## Act V, Part B.

(162 solid lines; word-average, .148)

No passages from Webster.

Passages from Dekker.

(a) *Northward Ho* V. B: Leap but into the saddle that now stands empty for you, you are made forever.

*Lanthorn and Candlelight*, p. 250: As by a mad sort of comrades whom I see leaping into the saddle, anon it will appear.

*Honest Whore II* IV. 1: The master no sooner lights but the man leaps into the saddle.

[All three of the above passages are metaphorical.]

(b) *Northward Ho* V. B: Look you, sir, there is as pretty a little pinnace struck sail hereby, and comes in lately: she's my kinswoman.

*Match Me in London* II:

> I hope your majesty
> Dare swear I ha' played the pilot cunningly,
> Fetching the wind about to make this pinnace
> Strike sail as you desired.  [*]

(c) *Northward Ho* V. B: Philip, this is your shuffling o' the cards, to turn up her for the bottom card at Ware.

*Match Me in London* IV: I did but shuffle the first dealing; you cut last and dealt last; by the same token you turned up a court card.

*Wonder of a Kingdom* V:

> Both how they shuffled, cut, and dealt about,
> What cards were best after the trumps were out,
> Who played false play, who true, who sought to save
> An ace i' the bottom, and turned up a knave.

(d) *Northward Ho* V. B: Pogs on you.
*Patient Grissil* IV. 2: A pogs on you.[1]  [?]

---

[1] Suggested by Bangs.

CHAPTER V.

## DIALECTIC AND METRICAL TESTS.

One trait of Dekker's, which is a matter of common knowledge to his readers, is his fondness for dialect and for phrases in modern languages. In this he is very different from Webster. Both authors quote Latin occasionally; but Webster never, I believe, certainly almost never, uses a phrase of French, German, Spanish, or Italian, although three of his plays are located in modern Italy, although Antonio has just come from France, and although Crispiano and Julio are Spaniards. Dekker, on the contrary, has the Dutch of the pretended Hans, the Welsh of Sir Owen and Sir Vaughn ap Rees, the Irish of Bryan in *The Honest Whore, Part II*, and of the disguised Andelocia in *Old Fortunatus*, the broken English of Angelo as a pretended French doctor in *The Wonder of a Kingdom*, the Spanish of Insultado in *Old Fortunatus*, &c. Consequently, we have every right to consider the presence of dialect passages, or phrases from a modern foreign language, as evidences of Dekker's work.

One such phrase, Honeysuckle's *que nouvelles*, is found in II. 1 of *Westward Ho*, and several Dutch phrases in II. 3 of the same play. Also in V. 4 we have Justiniano's *pardonnez-moi*. It is in *Northward Ho*, however, that this test is chiefly useful. Here the Dutch speeches of Hans van Belch and the Welsh of Captain Jenkins are prominent enough to form a considerable part of II. 1, IV. 1, IV. 2, and V. B.

The likeness between these speeches and the Dutch in *The Shoemaker's Holiday* or the Welsh in *Satiromastix* and *Patient Grissil* has already been pointed out,[1] and must be obvious to any reader.

Now it is certainly a significant fact that every scene in which these French or dialect speeches occur is a scene with a low word-average, and that the parallel passages for every one of these scenes are wholly from Dekker. In other words, we have here three different tests side by side, and all agreeing.

There is another form of test which, like the dialect one, applies to only a few scenes, but is very useful as far as it goes. II. 2 and IV. 2 in *Westward Ho*, and I. 3 in *Northward Ho* are partly in verse, and there are also a few lines of verse at the end of II. 1 in *Westward Ho*. Here we can apply metrical tests, and see whether they agree with the others.

In the passages from *Westward Ho* the versification is clearly that of Dekker. The masculine endings, and the regular, measured beat of the ten-syllable line, are typical of Dekker, and in marked contrast with Webster's frequent feminine endings, rugged transitions in the middle of the line, and numerous trisyllabic feet. The large amount of rime is also characteristic of Dekker, whereas Webster[2] uses rime

---

[1] See Bangs' remarks on this subject, *Engl. Stud.* 28. 218.

[2] The following table shows some of the chief features of Webster's metre. It is taken from E. E. Stoll's *John Webster*, p. 190, and is based on an examination of from 500 to 700 lines. For a discussion of Dekker's metre see the chapter on *Sir Thomas Wyatt* (see over).

| | Extra syllable, exclusive of epic cæsura | Feminine endings | Run-on lines | Rime |
|---|---|---|---|---|
| White Devil | 18.6 % | 31.4 % | 36.28 % | 4.5 % |
| Duchess of Malfi | 35.5 „ | 32.6 „ | 49.95 „ | 2.1 „ |
| Devil's Law Case | 29.8 „ | 32.6 „ | 35.8 „ | 1.03 „ |
| Appius and Virginia | 11.8 „ | 27.1 „ | 28.76 „ | 5.6 „ |
| Cure for a Cuckold | 10.9 „ | 19.5 „ | 28.88 „ | 1.17 „ |

sparingly. Like Dekker, also, are rimes between
different speeches, [1] and the rime of a short line with
a long one, or of a fragment of a line with a whole
one. Run-on lines are perhaps more common in these
scenes than in his plays as a whole, but no more
common than in many separate scenes.

A comparison of the following typical passages will
illustrate these various facts:

*Honest Whore I* V. 2:

> I have a hand, dear lord, deep in this act,
> For I foresaw this storm, yet willingly
> Put forth to meet it. Oft have I seen a father
> Washing the wounds of his dear son in tears,
> A son to curse the sword that struck his father,
> Both slain i' the quarrel of your families.
> Those scars are now ta 'en off; and I beseech you
> To seal our pardon! All was to this end,
> To turn the ancient hates of your two houses
> To fresh green friendship, that your loves might look
> Like the spring's forehead, comfortably sweet:
> And your vexed souls in peaceful union meet,
> Their blood will now be yours, yours will be theirs,
> And happiness shall crown your silver hairs.

*Westward Ho* IV. 2:

> Her body is the chariot of my soul,
> Her eyes my body's light, which if I want,
> Life wants, or if possess, I undo her,
> Turn her into a devil, whom I adore,
> By scorching her with the hot stream of lust.
> 'T is but a minute's pleasure, and the sin
> Scarce acted is repented: shun it, than:
> O, he that can abstain is more than man!
> Tush! Resolvest thou to do ill, be not precise:
> Who write of virtue best are slaves to vice.

---

[1] Practically all these metrical tests are from Mr. Stoll. See
his discussion of *Sir Thomas Wyatt*, pp. 52—54 of his *John Webster*.

The music sounds alarum to my blood:
What 's bad I follow, yet I see what 's good.

*Duchess of Malfi* III. 2:

Whate'er thou art that hast enjoyed my sister,
For I am sure thou hear'st me, for thine own sake
Let me not know thee.  I came hither prepared
To work thy discovery; yet am now persuaded
It would beget such violent effects
As would damn us both.  I would not for ten millions
I had beheld thee: therefore use all means
I never may have knowledge of thy name:
Enjoy thy lust still, and a wretched life
On that condition.—And for thee, vile woman,
If thou do wish thy lecher may grow old
In thy embracements, I would have thee build
Such a room for him as our anchorites
To holier use inhabit.  Let not the sun
Shine on him till he 's dead; let dogs and monkeys
Only converse with him, and such dumb things
To whom nature denies use to sound his name;
Do not keep a paraquito, lest she learn it;
If thou do love him, cut out thine own tongue,
Lest it bewray him.

In *Northward Ho* I. 3 the evidence is not so strong. There are fewer rimes and more feminine endings, and a large number of run-on lines.  Nevertheless the general movement of the verse is that of Dekker, and the differences noted above are only such as can be found in some of Dekker's scenes.  A special characteristic of Dekker which is not exactly a question of metre, but which comes in here most conveniently, is what Mr. Stoll calls his eruptive, sulphurous style. This is certainly shown in the scene in question.

The following passages seem to show that Dekker might have written this scene:

*Northward Ho* I. 3:

Villains, you have abused me, and I vow
Sharp vengeance on your heads!—Drive in your tears:
I take your word you 're honest; which good men,
Very good men, will scarce do to their wives.
I will bring home these serpents, and allow them
The heat of mine own bosom; wife, I charge you,
Set out your haviours toward them in such colours
As if you had been their whore; I 'll have it so.
I 'll candy o'er my words and sleek my brow,
Entreat 'em that they would not point at me,
Nor mock my horns: with this arm I 'll embrace 'em,
And with this—go to!

*Honest Whore* I II. 1:

You 're like the Jews, scattered, in no place certain,
Your days are tedious, your hours burdensome:
And were 't not for full suppers, midnight revels,
Dancing, wine, riotous meetings, which do drown
And bury quite in you all virtuous thoughts,
And on your eyelids hang so heavily,
They have no power to look so high as Heaven,—
You'd sit and muse on nothing but despair,
Curse that devil Lust, that so burns up your blood,
And in ten thousand shivers break your glass
For his temptation. Say you taste delight,
To have a golden gull from rise to set,
To mete you in his hot, luxurious arms,
Yet your nights pay for all: I know you dream
Of warrants, whips and beadles, and then start
At a door's windy creak; think every weasel
To be a constable, and every rat
A long-tailed officer: Are you now not slaves?
O, you 've damnation without pleasure for it.

*Satiro-mastix*, p. 198:

Say that you have not sworn unto your paper,
To blot her white cheeks with the dregs and bottom
Of your friends' private vices: say you swear

Your love and your allegiance to bright virtue
Makes you descend so low, as to put on
The office of an executioner,
Only to strike off the swoln head of sin,
Where'er you find it standing,
Say you swear;
And make damnation parcel of your oath,
That when your lashing jests make all men bleed,
Yet you whip none.   Court, city, country, friends,
Foes, all must smart alike; yet court, nor city,
Nor foe, nor friend, dare wink at you; great pity.

Mr. Stoll says, 'The verse in *Westward Ho* and *Northward Ho* is in every way like Dekker's.' I should qualify this statement by saying that the versification in *Westward Ho* is strong evidence for the theory of Dekker's authorship, and that that in *Northward Ho* is consistent with such a theory, but indeterminate as evidence.

Now if we look back, we shall find that every one of these scenes containing verse-passages is a scene with a low word-average, that each of them has a long list of parallel passages, and that these parallel passages are all from Dekker.   In other words, here again we have three different tests agreeing perfectly.

This fact is quite important, because the two Earl-scenes in *Westward Ho* contain the best literature in the three collaborated plays; and the question of their authorship is a vital question to every intelligent student of English literature.

## CHAPTER VI.

## THE INCIDENT-TEST.

Another form of evidence which is often very valuable is a similarity of incident between a collaborated and an uncollaborated play. This test is especially valuable in the case of authors who are known to have the habit of repeating incidents and situations in their various works. That Dekker is emphatically such a writer has already been pointed out by Mr. Stoll.[1] But if we examine Webster carefully, we shall find that he frequently does the same, although not to quite such an extent as Dekker; and consequently that parallel events and situations from either author, as well as parallel passages, can be accepted as strong evidence.

As an example of incident repeated in Webster, we may point to his law-court scenes. Three different plays of his—*The White Devil*, *The Devil's Law Case*, and *Appius and Virginia*—contain trial scenes. Moreover, in each of these scenes there is a spruce lawyer more eloquent than impressive. Again, both the scene in *The White Devil* and the scene in *The Devil's Law Case* start out by assigning a place to a prominent spectator (Brachiano and Ercole). In *The Devil's Law Case*, Contarino and Ercole come to court in disguise. In *Appius and Virginia*, Virginius and his daughter come in the dress of slaves, which is as near to a disguise as historical truth will permit. Both Vir-

[1] *John Webster*, pp. 71–72.

ginius and Vittoria plead to the court in their own
defense.

Another feature of Webster's work, which is partly
due, no doubt, to his school of the drama, but which
also shows his tendency to repeat incidents, is his
use of disguise. In *The White Devil*, Francisco de
Medecis disguises himself as a Moor to go to Brachiano's court. In *The Devil's Law Case*, Jolenta also
disguises herself as a Moor in her escape. In *The
White Devil*, Lodovico and Gasparo appear disguised
as friars. In *The Devil's Law Case*, Contarino and
Ercole disguise themselves as friars also.

Other instances might be cited. Both Brachiano
and the cardinal in *The Duchess of Malfi* are murdered
by one or two desperate men in their own palaces,
while their own friends are kept out of the room
through a misunderstanding. The last thing in both
*The White Devil* and *The Duchess of Malfi* is where
the son of the leading male character (Giovanni and
the son of Antonio) enters as the inaugurator of
a new *régime*. Other instances might be given; but
these are sufficient to show that Webster frequently
does repeat himself in incident and situation.

Now if we are to use these parallel circumstances,
as we may call them, to decide the authorship of
particular scenes, we must carefully confine ourselves to
events that happen wholly, or, at least, chiefly, within
those scenes. If Webster were writing an additional
scene for an existing play of Dekker's, it is obvious that
he would make the action of his part fit into the action
of the whole, and threads of movement which run
throughout the play would be incorporated into his work,
without proving in any way that he first conceived them.
For instance, Mr. Stoll implies that I. 1 in *Westward
Ho* was written by Dekker, because Justiniano, like Lacy

in *The Shoemaker's Holiday,* decides to lurk around London in disguise. But, this disguise of Justiniano's forms the backbone of the whole play, and runs through scene after scene. It is barely mentioned in the last speech of the opening scene, that is all; and this mention is not in any way a part of that scene itself, but simply the connecting link by which the author of that scene fastened his work to the rest of the play. In the same way, Mr. Stoll would give Act V of *Northward Ho* to Dekker, because the way in which the different characters assemble is very similar to the way in which they come together during the last act in both parts of *The Honest Whore.* But here again, this gathering is a movement which starts with Mayberry's proposal in IV. 1, and runs through almost two entire acts. Moreover, this assembling of all the *dramatis personæ* is not carried out in V. A, but in V. B. The chief thing in V. A is the trick by which Greenshield brings his own wife to his comrades unwittingly; and this is a wholly isolated event, conceived, carried out, and finished, all within the limits of that one scene. These parallels of Mr. Stoll's are very valuable in determining who planned this or that play as a complete whole, and that is really the only question which that writer is discussing; but they should not be applied to single scenes.

Now it must be said at the start that the incident-test is one which is very liable to abuse. The variety of expression in language is almost infinite; the possible variations in incident are quite limited; and consequently likenesses which are due to mere chance must be far more frequent in parallel incidents than in parallel passages. Then, too, the idea of stage-action is so indefinite, and depends so much on the

reader's interpretation, that the personal equation
enters far more than in a discussion of passages;
and this personal element, in the case of an enthusiastic
student, is liable to be prejudiced. However, in
the following pages I have tried to be as fair
and judicial as possible; and if at times I have
made mountains out of molehills, that is a small
matter, if at other times I have produced some trust-
worthy evidence. For the sake of clearness, I shall
take these plays up in order, scene by scene.

### Westward Ho.

I. 1.  There are so many bawds in Dekker's plays,
that we naturally think of them at the first appear-
ance of Birdlime.  Yet, if we examine all these interesting ladies in detail, we fail to find them in situations like that of Birdlime here.  The scenes introducing Madam Fingerlock and Madam Horseleech
have absolutely no connection.  The nearest parallel
in Dekker is Lady Dildoman in *Match Me in London*,
and Lady Dildoman acts as go-between for a king
and a citizen's wife, as Birdlime does for the Earl
and Mrs. Justiniano.  But, on examination the likeness
proves deceptive.  Lady Dildoman does not carry
any messages to Tormiella; on the contrary, she comes
with the king himself, and he does most of the talking.  Also, in the scene before Tormiella's house,
no jealous husband appears, no word about love is
said.  The king and his bawd come like respectable
people, chaffer for merchandise, and go away.  There
is a second scene at the king's palace, where Dildoman attempts to win over Tormiella to unchastity;
but this scene again has scarcely any likeness to
I. 1 in *Westward Ho*, although, as we shall point out
later, it has a very strong likeness to II. 2.  This

second scene in *Match Me in London* is at the lover's house; I. 1 is at the husband's; in this the lover is present with the bawd, and the husband is not there; in I. 1 the lover is not there, and the husband comes in; moreover, Tormiella is frightened and angry, while Mrs. Justiniano is half won over. In short, there is no scene in Dekker which shows even a plausible likeness to the one under discussion.

Now there is no very convincing parallel in Webster either; but I. 2 of *The White Devil* offers some rather interesting analogies. If we begin in this scene at page 12 of the Mermaid Edition, where Vittoria comes in and Camillo retires to the back of the stage, we have the following situation: The characters in the foreground are a bawd (Flamineo) and a citizen's wife (Vittoria). The bawd is tempting the woman to yield to the love of a great nobleman (Brachiano); and it is significant that both Birdlime and Flamineo tempt the woman with similar promises of soft beds and perfumed linen.[1] Then the husband (Camillo) comes forward, and we have the same trio as that in *Westward Ho*. True, he is not jealous now as Justiniano is, but he has been very jealous a few pages back, and has required a great deal of soothing down. Here the likeness stops, for, when the trio breaks up, the bawd and wife are left together instead of the husband and wife.

The above comparison is rather forced; I do not claim that it proves very much; but, as far as it goes, it certainly favors Webster rather than Dekker.

I. 2. In this scene Monopoly is making love to Mrs. Tenterhook, and at the same time carrying on pecuniary dealings with her husband, somewhat as

---

[1] See parallel passages, *Westward Ho* I. 1.

Laxton does with Mr. and Mrs. Gallipot in *The Roaring Girl* III. 2.[1] There is nothing at all like it in Webster.

II. 1.   This scene shows a rather striking similarity to II. 1 in the second part of *The Honest Whore*.   In *Westward Ho*, Justiniano, in the disguise of a school-master, talks for a while with Honeysuckle; he is then left alone with his wife, and gives her a letter from her lover.   In *The Honest Whore*, Orlando, in the disguise of a serving man, talks for a while with Matheo, and then is left alone with his wife, and gives her a message and a purse from her lover.   There is nothing in the least like it in Webster.

II. 2.   The early part of this scene bears some likeness to the second scene of Act II in *Match Me in London*.   In both, the characters engaged are a lover of high rank, a citizen's wife, and a bawd.   In both, the scene is at the lover's house.   In both, the bawd first, and later the lover, urges the woman to yield.   To be sure, Birdlime goes out while the Earl and Mrs. Justiniano are talking, whereas Lady Dildoman stays and helps out the king; but this lessens the parallelism without destroying it.

As regards the latter part of the scene, I will quote Mr. Stoll:

In *Westward Ho*, II, 2, a woman—Mrs. Justiniano—turns from her evil way, and, on the next approach of the bawd, curses her.   Exactly so in *The Honest Whore*, Pt. I, III, 2, the repentant Bellafront.

There is even a likeness in their words, as can be seen by referring to the parallel passages for this scene.

II. 3.   In this scene, the discussion about a trip and the decision to go to Brainford bear some like-

[1] From Stoll.

ness to II. 1 in *The Roaring Girl*, where Laxton and
Moll plan a trip to the same place.[1] In each case,
a *rendezvous* is appointed, the Greyhound in *Westward
Ho*, and Gray's Inn Fields in *The Roaring Girl*. The
device to have the child sick is found again in *The
Bachelor's Banquet*; but that has already been given
under the head of parallel passages.

III. 1. This dialogue of a wife and a husband, in
which the wife wheedles the husband into a scheme
by which she may privately see her lover, is very
much like the scene in chapter 8 of *The Bachelor's Banquet*,
p. 229. In *The Bachelor's Banquet*, the two are talking at night instead of in the daytime, and the precise
scheme is different; but the wheedling tone of the
wife, the good-natured but reluctant yielding of the
husband, and the woman's ultimate design of seeing
her lover privately, are common to both.

III. 2. For this scene, I quote from Mr. Stoll:[2]

In *Westward Ho*, III, 2, there is an arrest of a gallant
by Sergeant Ambush and his yeoman, Clutch; as in *Northward Ho*, II, 1, by two sergeants, as in *The Roaring Girl*
III, 3, by Sergeant Curtleaxe and Yeoman Hanger. In *The
Honest Whore*, Part I, IV, 3, moreover, Candido is arrested
by officers, and in Part II, Candido with others. In the first
instances the sergeants and yeomen are very like in character—important, and stern against evildoers.

Monopoly's attempt to escape by passing himself
off as one of the court also reminds us of a similar
device suggested in chap. 8 of *The Gull's Hornbook*.

The only thing which can possibly suggest this
incident in Webster is the part of the two lictors in
*Appius and Virginia* III. 2. But, although this scene
furnishes one very marked parallel passage, it shows

[1] Suggested by Stoll.
[2] *John Webster*, p. 72.

very little similarity in any other way.  In Webster, the lictors satirize society for a page or two, in a manner wholly unlike Ambush or Hanger; then they drop into the background, and have nothing to say or do when the actual arrest occurs.  Moreover, in Webster the person arrested is an innocent young girl, while in both *Westward Ho* and *The Roaring Girl* it is a gay young man about town.

III. 3.  This scene shows a number of surprising similarities to *The Devil's Law Case* III. 2.  In each the scene is a street before a house-door.  In each, the principal character comes on at the opening of the scene in disguise.  In each case this disguised person speaks with two people who come out of the house to meet him.  Justiniano comes to deliver a message, Romelio to make a proposal; but both come to talk with the inmates of the house on speccial errands, and the very length of the two conversations is about the same.  Again, each of these two men, Romelio and Justiniano, indulges in two long and rather abstract soliloquies; and, in each case, one of these soliloquies comes before his conversation with the people in the house, and the other after they have left him.  It is true that in *The Devil's Law Case* the audience are probably supposed to imagine a change of scene a few lines before the second soliloquy, since that appears to be spoken by Contarino's bed.  But the dialogue at the point of shift is so closely linked that it is impossible to treat it dramatically as two scenes.  Obviously this is one of those cases, rendered possible by Elizabethan stage-machinery, where the place was supposed to change, but the action was continuous.  Hence the two soliloquies of Romelio would fit in almost exactly like those of Justiniano.

Another important thing to notice is that Justiniano does not act the part of a collier. He says ' Buy any small coal' once or twice in a rather perfunctory way, tells the boy a story which may be amusing or satirical, as you please to take it, and spends the rest of the time in moralizing like an Othello. This is characteristic of Webster. He puts many characters in disguise, but he never makes them materially alter their character or speech in order to act their parts. For instances of this, turn to Francisco de Medicis as a Moor in *The White Devil*; Jolenta as a Moor, Contarino and Ercole as friars, in *The Devil's Law Case*; and Bosola as an old man in *The Duchess of Malfi*. On the contrary, the disguised characters of Dekker are perfect actors. Angelo in *The Wonder of a Kingdom* talks broken French, and chatters like a Gaul; Andelocia in *Old Fortunatus* hawks apples like a Yankee peddler, and talks unmistakable Irish; and Lacy in *The Shoemaker's Holiday* becomes so Dutch that we hardly recognize him ourselves.

Lastly, there is no disguise scene anywhere in Dekker in which the place is a street before a house, in which the disguised man comes to deliver a special message to those within, or in which the disguised man indulges in long moral soliloquies.

III. 4. For this scene, I have not been able to find anything worth while from either author.

IV. 1. This scene is like II. 1 in the First Part of *The Honest Whore* in that it represents a gathering of gallants at a strumpet's house; there is not much likeness in any other way. Tenterhook's attempt to steal away in the disguise of a scrivener, and his discovery in the process, bears a rather vague resemblance to the attempt of Hippolito, Infelice, and Matheo to escape as friars, and their discovery on the way out. Neither of the above parallelisms is very close. Webster has nothing at all similar.

IV. 2. For this scene I quote again from Mr. Stoll:[1]

In *Westward Ho*, IV, 2, the scene in the Earl's mansion, where Mistress Justiniano, the object of his lust, is discovered to him dead. Like *Satiro-mastix*, pp. 251–263. In both, the Earl (or King) had enticed the woman to his house; and now, bidding music sound, enters the room exultantly; but only suddenly to discover her poisoned, dead. In both, the husband avows the deed, and reproaches the libertine; the latter repents; and, the danger over, the woman, having taken only a sleeping potion, awakes. Like this, too, is the first scene in the *Honest Whore*, in which the Duke, seeking to thwart the love of Hippolito for his daughter, gives her out for dead, but, as he is conveying her body through the streets, is forced to set it down that the lover may see her face. She, too, recovers from the potion, and shortly after awakes. Like it, again, are both *Satiro-mastix* and *Match Me in London* in the matter of the seduction of the woman of lower rank to the libertine nobleman's house.

V. I. The way in which these citizens' wives come to Brainford, and then turn virtuous and fool their gallants, bears some likeness to the scheme of going to Brentford which was formed by the citizens' wives in *The Roaring Girl*,[2] and then given up when their better nature awakened. It was probably imitated from *Westward Ho*; but Dekker would be more liable to imitate his own work.

V. 2. This is merely a nominal scene of eight lines in Dyce's edition.

V. 3. I quote again from Stoll:[1]

In *Westward Ho*, V, 2, [V. 3 in Dyce's Edition], Sir Gosling's forcing the bawd to dance and sing is like Tucca's

---

[1] *John Webster*, p. 72.
[2] *Roaring Girl* IV. 2. Suggested by Stoll.

hazing of Horace and Asinius in *Satiro-mastix*.[1] In both the tyrant is drunk, and the frightened victims plead for mercy. Cf. *Satiro-mastix*, pp. 230 f., 234 f., 257 f. Similar is Bot's treatment of Candido, *Honest Whore*, Pt. II, IV, 3, and Candido's pleading.

V. 4. Justiniano's action in removing his false hair near the end of this scene is twice imitated in Dekker's later plays, once in *The Roaring Girl* IV. 2, and once in *The Honest Whore II* II. 3. In each case the accompanying speeches sound very much like those in *Westward Ho*, as can be seen by referring to the parallel passages. Of course, both of these incidents are imitations; but Dekker would be more apt to remember and imitate his own work, especially in the Second Part of *The Honest Whore*, which was probably written many years after *Westward Ho*.

## Northward Ho.

I. 1. The main incident of this scene was probably taken indirectly from an Italian *novella*,[2] and therefore not original with either Dekker or Webster. It is worthy of note, however, that an incident somewhat similar is used again in Webster's *Cure for a Cuckold* V. 1. In each case, a young gallant pretends that he has enjoyed the love of an innocent woman, and says that she has given him a jewel which was an especial love-token from her husband. In each case, the second statement has a certain amount of literal truth in it, although the accompanying implication is wholly false. The motives of the two men are different: Greenshield says plainly that he has enjoyed the woman's love, Rochfield only hints it, and Greenshield's statement is made to the woman's husband,

---

[1] Stoll took this from Fleay.

[2] See Stoll's *John Webster*, p. 63.

Rochfield's to a family friend; nevertheless, the similarity here seems too great for mere chance. I cannot find any corresponding parallel in Dekker.

I. 2.   For analogies to Philip's arrest see *Westward Ho* III. 2.

I. 3.   The central idea of this scene, a jealous husband accusing his wife, and the woman defending herself, is so common that parallels to it mean almost nothing.   There is a scene somewhat like it between Brachiano and Vittoria, *White Devil* IV. 1; and two or three such scenes are either mentioned or described in Dekker's *Bachelor's Banquet* (pages 209 and 223, for example); but none of these probably mean anything.

Philip comes in just out of prison, as Matheo does in *The Honest Whore II* II. 1, and as Plain Dealing[1] does in *The Whore of Babylon*, p. 212.   This favors Dekker as far as it goes, but the likeness is not very convincing.

II. 1.   On this scene Mr. Stoll has the following:

In *Northward Ho*, II, 1 (and after), a fiery Welsh captain woos Doll Hornet with something of the jealousy and fervour of rivalry to be found in the wooings of Sir Owen and Sir Vaughan ap Rees; and, again like Sir Owen, he promises her a coach and horses.

There is also a slight similarity between the way that Doll gulls Allum, and the way that the wives get money out of their husbands in *The Bachelor's Banquet* (chapter 1, for example).   Again, the procession of the three different types of lovers suggests somewhat the procession of the three different types of whores in the last scene of *The Honest Whore, Part II*.   In each case, the mildest individual comes in the middle, and the fieriest last.

---

[1] For similarity of words see parallel passages.

II. 2. There is some likeness between this scene and II. 4 of *The Cure for a Cuckold*. In *Northward Ho*, Greenshield introduces his wife into Mayberry's home, pretending that she is his sister. In *The Cure for a Cuckold*, Annabel introduces Rochfield into her father's house as a cousin of her husband. Neither Kate nor Rochfield wears any disguise; they are simply introduced under false names. Tibaldo Neri, in Dekker's *Wonder of a Kingdom*, is brought to Lord Vanni's house by Alphonsina as her sister instead of her brother; but Tibaldo puts on an elaborate disguise, changing his sex; and his introduction to the house is not shown on the stage.

III. 1. I quote again from Stoll:

In *Northward Ho*, III, 1, and IV, 4,[1] the trick of getting the respectable man, Bellamont, into the company of (a) whores and (b) madmen. Like it (a) in *Honest Whore*, Pt. II, IV, 3, and V, 2 is Candido's being inveigled into hobnobbing with the old bawd and Bots, forced to 'drink, dance, and sing bawdy songs,' and lodged among the whores at Bridewell, and (b) in Pt. I, IV, 3, and V, 2, his being carried off, amid protestations like Bellamont's, to Bedlam. In all these instances, it is practical joking and horseplay. In connection with this, there are, in both plays, mad-scenes of a like stamp, introduced as a sort of diversion. . . . In *Northward Ho*, III, 1, Bellamont's calling upon Doll becomes the cause, beyond his intention, of her falling in love with him and despising herself and her ways. So in the *Honest Whore*, Pt. I, II, 1 and IV, 1, Hippolito, calling upon Bellafront, converts her and unwittingly causes her to love him.[2]

---

[1] IV. 3, Dyce's Edition.

[2] Mr. Stoll has the following footnote: 'Doll is not exactly converted; but, in her rude way, she is at least disgusted with herself,—'O filthy rogue that I am,' p. 219, and at p. 232 she is humble and "will be clean."' In both cases, but more emphatically in that of Doll, love is the cause of the change.

III. 2. I cannot find any good parallel for this scene. However, the desire of the two prentices, Leapfrog and Squirrel, not to see their old master wronged, is very much like the spirit shown by George and Candido's other apprentices, when they think their master is abused (*Honest Whore I* III. 1).

IV. 1. Stoll has the following:

Thereupon, in *Northward Ho*, IV, 1, Doll comes to Bellamont's house, and, though he has just forbidden any visitors, forces her way to him, and passionately avows her love, only to be scorned and rejected. Exactly so in *Honest Whore*, IV, 1, Hippolito forbids callers, yet cannot keep out Bellafront, who avows her love and is rejected.

IV. 2. This scene is short and unimportant. There is so little action in it that no parallel incidents could be expected.

IV. 3. For what Mr. Stoll has to say about this scene, see *Northward Ho* III. 1.

Both Dekker and Webster have mad-scenes, Dekker in the last scene of *The Honest Whore, Part I*, and Webster in *The Duchess of Malfi* IV. 2. A comparison of these, however, with the scene in *Northward Ho* shows that the latter is far closer to Dekker. In both *The Honest Whore* and *Northward Ho* the mad folk are in their own madhouse; the other people come there, and the maniacs are brought in to furnish a pleasant diversion. In *The Duchess of Malfi*, the lunatics have been brought from their own home into the Duchess' apartments; and they are brought, not by her wish nor for her amusement, but to inspire her with terror. Moreover, the general atmosphere in Webster's scene is morbid and terrible, that in both of the other scenes light and comic.

V. A. In this, the idea of Greenshield's acting as pander for his own wife, even in jest, seems to me to have something repulsive and jarring in it. If this is so, it is evidence in favor of Webster's authorship. Webster is fond of abnormal incidents, which violate all our ideas of healthy family relations. For examples of this, turn to Flamineo as bawd for his own sister, the stupid Camillo persuaded out of the way for his own wife's dishonor, old Castrucchio fooled by his adulterous young wife, Leonora rival to her own daughter and throwing the stain of bastardy on her own son, Romelio anxious to ruin his own sister's good name, etc. On the contrary, Dekker, in spite of his fondness for introducing strumpets and scenes of debauchery, always treats the family with reverence. Even in the two most extreme cases—where Matheo in *The Honest Whore* wishes to turn his wife whore again for profit, and where Tibaldo Neri in *The Wonder of a Kingdom* urges his sister to act as bawd for him—the temporary baseness of the men only brings into sharper relief the virtuous indignation of Bellafront and the horror-stricken reproaches of Alphonsina.

The arrival of Kate and Greenshield in disguise, and the discovery of Kate, is, on the whole, more like Webster. The closest parallel in Dekker is the discovery of the three supposed friars in their flight from Bedlam (last scene of *Honest Whore, Part I*). But here the people are trying to slip away and are intercepted, while in *Northward Ho* they come on purpose to meet the crowd, and join them voluntarily. In *The Devil's Law Case* V. 6, Jolenta, in the disguise of a Moor, is brought in by two surgeons, one dressed like a Jew, and discovers herself before her relatives and friends. Here, as in *Northward Ho*, the two disguised people come on purpose to join the crowd. Again, in *Northward Ho* we have the idea of two disguised people who are familiar friends meeting without knowing each other. So in *The Devil's Law Case* V. 2, Ercole and Contarino, both in the disguise of friars, are talking together, and Ercole does not know who Contarino is.

Of course, the final removal of the false hair and beard, and the words 'Behold the parenthesis,' were suggested by the end of *Westward Ho*; but it should be noticed that neither the action nor the words at this point are as close to *Westward Ho* as they are in either *The Roaring Girl* IV. 2, or *The Honest Whore II* II. 3. In *Northward Ho*, others pull off the disguise, and there is no similarity of language; in all the other three scenes the man himself pulls off his false hair, and there is considerable likeness in the language, as can be seen by referring to the parallel passages.

Lastly, it may be worth while to compare the way in which Bellamont persuades the stupid Greenshield to pander his own wife to them with the manner in which Flamineo persuades the equally stupid Camillo to get out of the way when Brachiano is coming to his wife.

V. B.   I quote again from Stoll:

In *Northward Ho*, V, 1 [Part B according to my division], Doll suddenly contents herself at the end with another, inferior mate, who is entangled into marriage with her, through no fault of hers, by a trick. Likewise in *Honest Whore*, Part I, V, 2, Bellafront and Matheo.

## CHAPTER VII.

# THE CHARACTER- AND ATMOSPHERE-TEST.

The last test to be applied is that found in the general atmosphere of the various scenes, and in the character-study of the leading *dramatis personæ*. This is obviously the most impressionistic, the least rigorously scientific, of all our tests, and consequently the most liable to be biased by personal prejudice. Nevertheless, its value is unquestionable, since it takes into consideration certain factors which the other *criteria* fail to note; and, if every impression is critically compared with the material which inspired it, the test may be made more scientific than seems at first to be possible.

We have the peculiar advantage in this case of being able to call on an unprejudiced witness. Mr. Stoll has already made a careful study of this test from the side of Dekker, and has embodied it in a short but pithy discussion. As he knew nothing of either my word-test or my parallel passages, he would be wholly free from bias. For this reason, I quote his remarks *verbatim*:

The gallants,[1] citizens, and citizens' wives, whores and bawds, Welshmen and Dutchmen, are probably all Dekker's; for they all appear in previous plays, such as the *Shoemaker*, *Satiro-mastix*, and the *Honest Whore*, as well as in his later ones. They appear in *none* of Webster's, whether comedy or tragedy.

A few of these types—those that present much individuality—we will examine a little more closely. The citizens'

---

[1] *John Webster*, p. 74, f.

wives, the bawds, and the whores are done in a striking
style, in continuation, perhaps, of Shakespeare's types,—the
Merry Wives, Mrs. Quickly and Doll Tearsheet. Dekker's
they are, at all events, through and through, and, as present-
ed both in our comedies and in Dekker's other works, they
have much in common. All three—citizen's wife, whore,
and bawd—affect virtue, speak of it freely and complacently,
bridle up at any infringement of what they call the proprieties or their own dignity, are coarse, in fair weather
goodnatured, and naïve. The citizens' wives—Tenterhook,
Honeysuckle, and Wafer in *Westward Ho*, as well as Gallipot,
Tiltyard, and Openwork in the *Roaring Girl*,—the whores
—Doll Hornet in *Northward Ho* as well as Bellafront in the
*Honest Whore*—swear by their virtue, and all, even the last
named, make much ado at the last moment to defend it.
The bawds and whores are incensed when given their titles,
and Mrs. Birdlime in *Westward Ho*, like Mistress Horseleech
in the *Honest Whore*, considers a bawd not a bawd at all,
but an honest, motherly woman. And one and all, not
omitting the citizenesses, Mistress Minever in *Satiro-mastix*
and Margery in the *Shoemaker*, are still more insistent on
the minor proprieties—will not abide the coarseness and
boisterousness of men, as drunkenness, tobacco-smoking, and
spitting, ' swaggering,' ' conjuring,' or unseasonable familiarity.
A rude and laughable prudishness marks them all, whether
of foul name or fair name, both in our comedies and in
Dekker's other plays.

The whores, like Doll Hornet and Lucy (to compare
Dekker's types with the representatives in our plays), are
given to Billingsgate and bravado, to loud anger and to
striking. The citizens' wives, like those in *Westward Ho*,
are given to naïve blundering and Partingtonism, to merriment
and larks, to playing the game with a gallant to the last
moment and then virtuously and indignantly bilking him.
Characteristic, indeed, of both citizens' wives and whores,
whether in our comedies or elsewhere in Dekker, is this
wheeling about at the end: the citizens' wives undergo a
sudden alteration, and help one another to cheat the

gallants, as in *Westward Ho* and the *Roaring Girl*; and
the whores (including Mistress Justiniano [who almost becomes one]) fall really in love and by their love are converted, curse the bawd, and take on a new, unworldly tone,
as do Doll Hornet and Bellafront. And as for the bawds,
they, like Birdlime, are most jealous of their reputation,
scandalized at the mere word bawd, 'honest and motherly,'
and greatly given to *aqua vitæ* and tricks of the trade. All
these coarse-grained, loud, and jolly women, then, are of
one flock, and that is Dekker's.

Manifestly, Dekker's, too, are the Dutch Drawer and Merchant, and the Welsh Captain. A Dutch Hans had already
appeared in the *Shoemaker*, as well as a Dutch skipper;
and Captain Jenkins in *Northward Ho* is, in the character
of his Cambrian English and blunders, his generosity, the
ardor of his suit for a woman's hand, his pugnacity and
ready, childlike placability, the counterpart of Sir Vaughan
ap Rees in *Satiro-mastix*.

Such is the testimony of Stoll. Now let us see
what scenes he would assign to Dekker according to
character and atmosphere. The three citizens, their
wives, and their wives' gallants form the main part
of I. 2; II. 1; II. 3; III. 1; III. 2; III. 4; IV. 1; V. 1;
V. 4. (Honeysuckle and his wife appear for only
a moment in III. 3, and their speeches then give us
the only trace of Dekker's hand in the whole scene.)
The whores include *Westward Ho* IV. 1, and *Northward Ho* I. 2; II. 1; III. 1; IV. 1; V. B. All Stoll's
remarks about Birdlime are based on incidents in
II. 2 and IV. 1 of *Westward Ho*. The remarks about
Mrs. Justiniano are based wholly on II. 2. The Dutch
Drawer appears in *Westward Ho* II. 3; the Dutch
Merchant in *Northward Ho* II. 1. Captain Jenkins
takes part in II. 1; IV. 1; IV. 2; and V. B in *Northward Ho*. In other words, every incident or bit of
evidence given above by Mr. Stoll is from some scene

which our previous tests had assigned to Dekker (except *Northward Ho* III. 1, in which the word-test and parallel-passage test proved inconclusive either way).

Again, Mr. Stoll goes on to point out that Dekker, more than any other Elizabethan dramatist, was a London man, full of allusions to her customs, her social resorts, and local geography, and that this element in *Westward Ho* and *Northward Ho* is proof of his authorship. Now the scenes which show this the most in their references to Charing Cross, St. Paul's, Lambeth Marsh, the various taverns of London, etc., are *Westward Ho* II. 1; II. 3; IV. 1; and *Northward Ho* I. 2. All of these are scenes which our previous tests had assigned to Dekker.

It is true that Mr. Stoll sees something Dekkerian in the jealousy of Justiniano, *Westward Ho* I. 1 and III. 3, and that of Mayberry, *Northward Ho* I. 1 and I. 3; but, on reading carefully, we find that he is basing his conclusion for all these scenes on the incidents in *Northward Ho* I. 3, as they rose to his memory; and *Northward Ho* I. 3 is an unmistakable Dekker scene. On the whole, then, the character- and atmosphere-test seems to work out satisfactorily as regards Dekker. Now let us turn to Webster.

The first noticeable thing in the scenes which we have hitherto assigned chiefly to Webster is their comparative lack of mirth. *Northward Ho* V. A is the only one of these five scenes which makes much attempt at fun; and even here the joke is rather heavy and clumsy; we miss Dekker's bubbling wit, clever little turns of speech, and general lightness of touch. *Westward Ho* I. 1 and III. 3, and *Northward Ho* I. 1 and II. 2, make almost no pretense of being amusing.

Another noticeable thing about all these scenes is the element of suppressed passion in them. Few of

Dekker's scenes contain violent passion at all; and
when they do—as in *Westward Ho* IV. 2, where Justiniano denounces the Earl, or in *Northward Ho* I. 3,
where Mayberry accuses his wife—that passion blazes
out openly at white heat, spends itself by its own
violence, and reacts in a reconciliation. But in the
Webster scenes there is a pent-up element which is
wholly different. Justiniano in *Westward Ho* I. 1 is
not declamatory, like Mayberry in *Northward Ho*
I. 3, but lowering, bitter, sarcastic. In *Northward Ho*
II. 2, Mayberry is welcoming his guests with hypo-
critical politeness, while he is training them on to
their own misfortune, and bids his wife welcome
them even if she wishes their throats cut. In *Northward Ho* V. A, when Greenshield becomes convinced
that he is made a cuckold, he utters only a few
short, bitter sentences, and apparently is spending the
rest of the time in pent-up savage brooding. So in the
other works of Webster we find polite and smiling
treachery on every hand, while most of Dekker's characters are frank and outspoken in either love or hate.

Now when we were examining the word-test, we
found some very profitable results from tracing the
same character from scene to scene. This may
prove profitable in the character-test also. Let us
begin with the character of the old bawd, Birdlime.
Dekker has several bawds, Madame Fingerlock and
Madame Horseleech in *The Honest Whore*, and Lady
Dildoman in *Match Me in London*. A comparison of
these ladies with Birdlime shows that she speaks very
much like them in *Westward Ho* II. 2; II. 3; IV. 1; and
V. 4; but that she does not seem at all like them in
I. 1. Take, for example, the following speech from I. 1:

Name you any one thing that your citizen's wife comes
short of to your lady: they have as pure linen, as choice

painting. . . . Your citizen's wife learns nothing but fopper-
ies of your lady; but your lady or justice-o'-peace madam
carries high wit from the city,—namely, to receive all and
pay all, to awe their husbands, to check their husbands,
to control their husbands; nay, they have the trick on 't
to be sick for a new gown, or a carcanet, or a diamond,
or so.

And again:

I have heard he loved you, before you were married,
entirely: what of that? I have ever found it most true in
mine own experience, that they which are most violent
dotards before their marriage are most voluntary cuckolds
after. Many are honest, either because they have not wit,
or because they have not opportunity, to be dishonest; and
this Italian, your husband's countryman, holds it impossible
any of their ladies should be excellent witty, and not make
the uttermost use of their beauty.

These are not the speeches of one of Dekker's
bawds. The bawds of Dekker are vulgar, narrow-
minded women, with a fulsome benevolence, and
a strict eye to business. They never trouble themselves about the abstract evils of society, but are
wholly absorbed in their *aqua vitæ*, their prospective
customers, and maintaining their own reputation for
maternal benevolence. The bitter, abstract social
satire of the above speeches is exactly what we find
in the speeches of Flamineo and Bosola. Compare,
for example, the following:

*White Devil* V. 1: FLAMINEO. Lovers' oaths are like
mariners' prayers, uttered in extremity; but when the tem-
pest is o'er, and that the vessel leaves tumbling, they fall
from protesting to drinking. And yet, amongst gentlemen,
protesting and drinking go together, and agree as well as
shoemakers and Westphalia bacon; they are both drawers-
on; for drink draws on protestation, and protestation draws
on more drink.

*Duchess of Malfi* I. 1 : Bosola.   Ay, to hang in a fair pair of slings, take his latter swing in the world upon an honourable pair of crutches, from hospital to hospital.   Fare ye well, sir; and yet do not you scorn us; for places in this court are but like beds in the hospital, where this man's head lies at that man's foot, and so lower and lower.

Turning now to *Westward Ho* II. 2, we find that there Birdlime talks in a wholly different strain, very much like that of Dekker's 'motherly' ladies.   The following passages illustrate this:

*Westward Ho* II. 2 : Birdlime.   O, I thought I should fetch you: you can 'ha' at that; I'll make you hem anon. As I 'm a sinner, I think you 'll find the sweetest, sweetest bedfellow of her.   O, she looks so sugaredly, so simperingly, so gingerly, so amorously, so amiably!   Such a red lip, such a white forehead, such a black eye, such a full cheek, and such a goodly little nose, now she's in that French gown, Scotch falls, Scotch bum, and Italian head-tire, you sent her, and is such an enticing she-witch, carrying the charms of your jewels about her!   O!

*Honest Whore I* III. 2 : Mrs. Fingerlock.   And had she no time to turn honest but now?   what a vile woman is this!   twenty pound a night, I 'll be sworn, Roger, in good gold and no silver: why, here was a time!   if she could ha' picked out a time, it could not be better: gold enough stirring; choice of men, choice of hair, choice of beards, choice of legs, and choice of every, every, everything: it cannot sink into my head, that she should be such an ass. Roger, I never believe it.

*Match Me in London* I: Lady Dildoman.   Delicate, piercing eye, inchanting voice, lip red and moist, skin soft and white; she's amorous, delicious, inciferous, tender, neat. . . . New married, that's all the hole you can find in her coat, but so newly, the poesie of her wedding ring is scarce warm with the heat of her finger; therefore my lord, fasten this wagtail, as soon as you can lime your bush, for women are Venice glasses, one knock spoils 'em.

The above extracts are all fairly representative passages; any one who doubts this may read and see; and they seem to speak for themselves.

Again, in *Westward Ho* I. 1 and III. 3, Justiniano not only seems much more violently jealous than he does elsewhere, but he also seems more typically Italian. In the Dekker scenes he talks very much like an English schoolmaster, and speaks to his wife in IV. 2 like a middle-class English husband. He scarcely ever alludes to his family troubles in these scenes. Even his soliloquy at the end of II. 1 shows scarcely any personal bitterness. Rather he seems to adopt a sort of quizzical contemplative attitude toward the frailty of the weaker sex in general; and he ends up with the consoling philosophy that

> If, as ivy round the elm does twine,
> All wives love clipping, there's no fault in mine.

In both of the Webster scenes, on the contrary, he is an Italian, and a jealous Italian, brooding, not over the abstract weakness of women in general, but over the rankling sore of his own domestic troubles.

This same examination cannot be pursued so profitably in *Northward Ho*, since there are no equally pronounced characters in that play which take any important part in the scenes of both authors. From what has been said above, however, it can be seen that the results of character- and general atmosphere-analysis agree at least reasonably well with the results of our other tests.

## CHAPTER VIII.

# CONCLUSIONS AS TO THE CITIZEN-COMEDIES.

The results of the various tests discussed in the preceding chapters are summarized in the table which I give below. In this table, the letter W under a certain test means that that test favors the authorship of Webster in that scene; in the same way D means that the authorship of Dekker is indicated. W > D means Webster's share greater than Dekker's, and D > W the opposite. W & D means that the test indicates the presence of both authors, without giving any definite idea as to their relative shares. Where the evidence for an author is weak and inconclusive, the letter representing his part is followed by an interrogation mark, as W ?. Where the evidence is unusually strong, the letter is followed by an exclamation mark, as D! Under the character- and atmosphere-test, evidence originating with myself is represented by a small letter—as w—in order that allowance may be made for prejudice in a largely impressionistic test. Since Stoll and other writers knew nothing of my word-test or parallel passages, an agreement between the atmosphere-test in their hands and the other tests in mine is about as significant as an agreement between two purely scientific tests.

## Westward Ho

| Scene | Word-test | Parallel passage-test[1] | Dialect-test | Metrical tests | Incident-test | Character- and atmosphere-test | Conclusions |
|---|---|---|---|---|---|---|---|
| I. 1. | .307 | W > D | — | — | W ? | w | W > D |
| 2. | .215 | W ? & D | — | — | D | D | D > (W ?) |
| II. 1. | .169 | D ! | D ? | D ? | D | D | D |
| 2. | .148 | D ! | — | D | D | D | D |
| 3. | .155 | D | D | — | D | D | D |
| III. 1. | .250 | D | — | — | D ? | D | D |
| 2. | .234 | W & D | — | — | D | D | D > W |
| 3. | .333 | W > D | — | — | W ! | w | W > D |
| 4. | .215 | D | — | — | — | D | D ? |
| IV. 1. | .169 | D | — | — | D ? | D | D |
| 2. | .149 | D | — | D | D ! | D | D |
| V. 1. | .200 | D | — | — | D | D | D |
| 2. | | | | | | | |
| 3. | .119 | D ! | — | — | D | D | D |
| 4. | .169 | D | D | — | D | D | D |

It will be seen that, although the tests given above modify and correct each other, they never sharply disagree, and usually support each other strongly. Such agreement between five or six different tests, some of them worked out by different men, ignorant

---

[1] It may seem as if the results of the parallel-passage test would be prejudiced, on the ground that a man would notice only such passages as he desired. But I have tried to be as careful and impartial as possible in this search. As an evidence of this, I can point to the fact that I religiously recorded three or four very doubtful parallels from Webster against *Northward Ho I.* 3, a scene with a word-average of .100; and afterwards found closer parallels from Dekker for the se very passages. Again, I did not hit on the idea of dividing *Northward Ho* V into two parts until after all my passages had been collected. I had supposed the whole was largely Webster's, and had been hunting high and low to find parallels to it. Yet, when I came to divide the act, all the parallels from Webster went to Part A.

of each other's conclusions at the time—such agreement cannot be the result of chance.

### Northward Ho

| Scene | Word-test | Parallel passage-test | Dialect-test | Metrical tests | Incident-test | Character- and atmosphere-test | Conclusions |
|---|---|---|---|---|---|---|---|
| I. 1. | .301 | W > D | — | — | W | w ? | W > D |
| 2. | .185 | D | — | — | D | D | D |
| 3. | .100 | D | — | D ? | D ? | D | D |
| II. 1. | .078 | D | D | — | D | D | D |
| 2. | .313 | W > D | — | — | W ? | w | W > D |
| III. 1. | .276 | W ? & D | — | — | D | D | W & D |
| 2. | .183 | D | — | — | — | d ? | D |
| IV. 1. | .223 | D ! | D | — | D | D | D |
| 2. | .179 | D | D | — | — | D | D |
| 3. | .107 | D | — | — | D | D | D |
| V. A. | .341 | W & D | — | — | W ? | w | W > D |
| V. B. | .148 | D | D | — | D | D | D |

On the strength of the evidence summarized in the above tables, we can form the following conclusions for *Westward Ho* and *Northward Ho* :

(a) Dekker was the guiding spirit in both plays.

(b) The hand, or at least the influence, of Dekker can be definitely traced in every single scene of both plays.

(c) Webster certainly wrote a considerable part, and probably by far the larger part, of *Westward Ho* I. 1 and III. 3 ; and of *Northward Ho* I. 1, II. 2, and V. A ; he also apparently had some part, probably a small one, in *Westward Ho* I. 2 and III. 2.

(d) *Northward Ho* III. 1 is an uncertain scene, probably written by Dekker, and retouched by Webster.

(e) Practically all the rest of both plays is the work of Dekker.

(f) Everything of real literary value in both plays, whether serious or comic, belongs to Dekker.

(g) Webster has not shown in these plays any ability as a humorist, or manysidedness, or literary trait of any kind, which is different from the Webster of the later plays.

(h) His small part in both of these plays, his small part in Marston's *Malcontent*, as shown by Stoll, and his own statements about the slowness with which he composed, would combine to make us suspect that his part in the lost collaborated plays was not large.

CHAPTER IX.

SIR THOMAS WYATT.

I cannot find that *Sir Thomas Wyatt* has ever yet been divided into scenes. As such a division is necessary at the very beginning of a discussion like the present, I have made the one given below. The numbers of the pages are those of Dyce's *Webster*.

Scene I, p. 185, ' How fares the king, my lord?' ... p. 186, ' Her royal name that must in state be crowned.'

Scene II, p. 186, ' Our cousin king is dead.' ... p. 187, ' Where prisoners keep their cave.'

Scene III, p. 187, ' Thus like a nun, not like a princess born.' ... p. 187, ' And for the daughter I through death will run.'

Scene IV, p. 187, ' Where 's Captain Brett?' ... p. 188, ' 'T is more than time, my friends, that we were gone.'

Scene V, p. 188, ' What, ho, porter, open the gate.' ... p. 188, ' Is these strange turmoils' wisest violence.'

Scene VI, p. 188, ' Though your attempt, lord treasurer' ... p. 190, ' And if the dukes be cross, we 'll cross their powers.'

Scene VII, p. 190, ' Lancepersado, quarter, quarter.' ... p. 190, ' My anchor is cast, and I in harbour ride.'

Scene VIII, p. 190, ' My lord, 't is true, you sent unto the council.' ... p. 192, ' My soul hath peace, and I embrace my end.'

Scene IX, p. 192, ' Three days are past' ... p. 193, ' A hundred pound, it weighs so heavy.'

Scene X, p. 193, 'By God's assistance, and the power of heaven' ... p. 195, 'To save the country, and this realm defend.'

Scene XI, p. 195, 'Good morrow to the partner of my woe, ... p. 196, 'My Dudley, my own heart.'

Scene XII, p. 196, 'Hold, drum! Stand, gentlemen!' ... p. 197, 'Be Englishmen, and beard them to their faces.'

Scene XIII, p. 197, 'Yonder the traitor marcheth' ... p. 198, 'You shall all be Lord Mayors at least.'

Scene XIV, p. 198, 'Those eight brass pieces shall do service now' ... p. 199, 'As e'er did faithful subject to his prince.'

Scene XV, p. 199, 'Pembroke revolts and flies to Wyatt's side.' ... p. 199, 'I hope for nothing, therefore nothing fear.'

Scene XVI, p. 199, 'My lord of Norfolk, will it please you sit? ... p. 201, 'Least griefs speak louder when the great are dumb.'

Scene XVII, p. 201, 'The sad aspect this prison doth afford' ... p. 204, 'Their fathers' pride their lives hath severéd.'

Now it may as well be said at the outset that the evidence which I have gathered for *Sir Thomas Wyatt* is far more meagre than that for either of the prose plays. In the first place, most of the scenes are very short; and this, while it does not render the word-test worthless, by any means, nevertheless makes it less reliable in those scenes. In the second place, the incident-test and the parallel-passage test prove weak through sheer lack of material. In both cases this is probably due to the fact that the play is a perfunctory task, which does not represent the real genius of either author. In the third place, the metrical tests, on which I had depended very much, usually prove disappointingly noncommittal in either direction. However, such evidence as I have is given below; and, although perhaps it seldom reaches the height of practical certainty, it throws more or less light on the authorship of nearly every scene.

Applying the word-test, we have the following results:

### *Sir Thomas Wyatt.*

| Scene. | Sold lines. | Words. | Average. |
|--------|-------------|--------|----------|
| I | 51 | 13 | .255 |
| II | 48 | 17 | .354 |
| III | 37 | 7 | .189 |
| IV | 38 | 9 | .237 |
| V | 26 | 12 | .461 |
| VI | 89 | 32 | .360 |
| VII | 28 | 5 | .178 |
| VIII | 95 | 22 | .232 |
| IX | 66 | 12 | .182 |
| X | 135 | 53 | .392 |
| XI | 48 | 13 | .271 |
| XII | 75 | 14 | .187 |
| XIII | 70 | 10 | .143 |
| XIV | 42 | 12 | .286 |
| XV | 28 | 1 | .036 |
| XVI | 118 | 54 | .458 |
| XVII | 136 | 28 | .206 |

It will be seen that the word-average of *Sir Thomas Wyatt* is in general higher than that of either of the prose comedies. This is partly explained by the subject-matter. The pompous ceremonial of palaces and law-courts naturally encourages the use of long Latin words. But if we make a little allowance for this, and say that all scenes below .240 must be Dekker's, all scenes above .350 Webster's, we have only three scenes in the wide indeterminate region between, and every one of these scenes is quite short. Every scene in the play containing as many as 60 solid lines—below which length the word-test is never very reliable—is either above .359 or below .233.

Now let us take up the various metrical tests. The features of Webster's mature verse-structure in which he differs most sharply from Dekker are: (a) A high percentage of run-on lines; (b) a high percentage of feminine endings; (c) a fondness for frequent tri-syllabic feet within the line; (d) a very sparing use of rime. Now, if we look in *Sir Thomas Wyatt* for the versification of the Webster whom we know, there is not a single scene in which we can find it. There is not a scene which contains any number of trisyllabic feet;[1] there is not a single scene which contains anything like so high a percentage of run-on lines as the lowest of Webster's plays. Moreover the average of rime is higher, and the average of feminine endings lower, in every single scene than in the general average of Webster's verse.

Now does this mean, as Mr. Stoll seems to imply, that Dekker wrote practically the whole play? I think not. We must remember that Webster at this time was a crude beginner, who probably had not yet formed his style of versification. *Sir Thomas Wyatt* was probably written some three years before *Westward Ho*, and some eight or ten years before *The White Devil*, the first of Webster's great tragedies. We know that many writers used masculine endings and end-stopped lines during their apprenticeship, and grew out of this habit later. If we assume that Webster changed half as much in those ten years as

---

[1] I have not made any table of this, but the fact is patent to any reader.

Shakespeare is known to have changed, we could feel free to credit him with certain scenes in the play before us. Consequently, in assigning scenes to Webster by metrical tests, we should try to find passages which do not look too much like Dekker, rather than such as will have any very close likeness to Webster's mature work.

With this caution in mind, let us turn to the following table:

*Metrical Table for Sir Thomas Wyatt.*

| Scene | Lines of verse | Number of riming lines | Number of run-on lines | Number of feminine endings | No. of couplets 1 long, 1 short line | Riming couplets of full length but with strong pause just before 1st or 2d rime | Rime between two speeches | Solid lines | Word-average |
|---|---|---|---|---|---|---|---|---|---|
| I | 65 | 14, or 21.5 % | 10, or 15.4 % | 13, or 20 % | 2 | 2 | 0 | 51 | .255 |
| II | 60 | 6, or 10 „ | 10, or 16.7 „ | 13, or 21.7 „ | 1 | 1 | 1 | 48 | .354 |
| III | 45 | 12, or 26.7 „ | 5, or 11.1 „ | 9, or 20 „ | 1 | 1 | 0 | 37 | .189 |
| IV | 45 | 14, or 31.1 „ | 9, or 20 „ | 2, or 4.4 „ | 0 | 4 | 0 | 38 | .237 |
| V | 32 | 8, or 25 „ | 4, or 12.5 „ | 4, or 12.5 „ | 1 | 0 | 1 | 26 | .461 |
| VI | 107 | 14, or 13.1 „ | 15, or 14 „ | 3, or 2.8 „ | 1 | 1 | 0 | 89 | .360 |
| VII | 13[1] | 8, or 61.5 „ | 0 | 0 | 1 | 1 | 0 | 28 | .178 |
| VIII | 111 | 24, or 21.6 „ | 12, or 10.8 „ | 21, or 18.9 „ | 4 | 4 | 1 | 95 | .232 |
| IX | 69 | 20, or 29 „ | 8, or 11.6 „ | 5, or 7.2 „ | 0 | 1 | 0 | 66 | .182 |
| X | 160 | 10, or 6.3 „ | 17, or 10.6 „ | 32, or 20 „ | 0 | 0 | 0 | 135 | .392 |
| XI | 56 | 14, or 25 „ | 3, or 5.4 „ | 7, or 12.5 „ | 0 | 0 | 0 | 48 | .271 |
| XII | 99 | 20, or 20.2 „ | 12, or 13.2 „ | 9, or 9.9 „ | 0 | 2 | 0 | 75 | .187 |
| XIII | 16[1] | 2, or 12.5 „ | 5, or 31.3 „ | 1, or 6.3 „ | 0 | 0 | 0 | 70 | .143 |
| XIV | 48 | 4, or 8.3 „ | 2, or 4.2 „ | 5, or 10.4 „ | 0 | 0 | 0 | 42 | .286 |
| XV | 37 | 16, or 43.3 „ | 6, or 16.2 „ | 1, or 2.7 „ | 2 | 4 | 0 | 28 | .036 |
| XVI | 122 | 32, or 26.2 „ | 2, or 1.6 „ | 9, or 7.4 „ | 0 | 4 | 5 | 118 | .458 |
| XVII | 162 | 76, or 46.9 „ | 9, or 5.5 „ | 11, or 6.7 „ | 1 | 5 | 5 | 136 | .206 |

Now let us compare the figures for Webster's later plays, and for three of Dekker's plays which are closest in time to *Sir Thomas Wyatt*.

---

[1] The verse part of these scenes is so small that the metrical results in them can have little value.

*Webster.*[1]

|  | Rime [2] | Run-on lines | Feminine endings |
|---|---|---|---|
| White Devil | 4.50 % | 36.28 % | 31.4 % |
| Duchess of Malfi | 2.1 „ | 49.95 „ | 32.6 „ |
| Devil's Law Case | 1.03 „ | 35.8 „ | 32.6 „ |
| Appius and Virginia | 5.6 „ | 28.76 „ | 27.1 „ |
| Cure for a Cuckold | 1.17 „ | 28.88 „ | 19.5 „ |

The three plays of Dekker's which are most in point in this discussion are *Fortunatus*, *The Whore of Babylon*, and *The Honest Whore, Part I*. All of these were nearly contemporary with *Sir Thomas Wyatt*, and all contain a large amount of verse.[3] In order to be sure of our ground, we will take these plays up scene by scene, as we did in the word-test, omitting a few scenes which are wholly or largely prose.

*Honest Whore, Part I.*

| Scene | Lines of verse | Feminine endings | Run-on lines | Riming lines |
|---|---|---|---|---|
| I. 1 | 92 | 8, or 8.7% | 26, or 28.2% | 12, or 13 % |
| I. 3 | 97 | 11, or 11.3 „ | 20, or 20.6 „ | 8, or 8.2 „ |
| I. 5 (end) | 30 | 8, or 26.7 „ | 4, or 13.3 „ | 12, or 40 „ |
| II. 1 (end) | 211 | 31, or 14.7 „ | 35, or 16.6 „ | 52, or 24.6 „ |
| III. 1 (end) | 82 | 7, or 8.5 „ | 5, or 6.1 „ | 18, or 22 „ |
| III. 2 | 19 | 9, or 47.4 „ | 3, or 15.8 „ | 0 |
| III. 3 | 70 | 12, or 17.1 „ | 13, or 18.6 „ | 28, or 40 „ |
| IV. 1 | 131 | 17, or 13 „ | 16, or 12.2 „ | 46, or 35.1 „ |
| IV. 4 | 107 | 10, or 9.3 „ | 17, or 15.9 „ | 26, or 24.3 „ |
| V. 1 | 34 | 5, or 14.7 „ | 9, or 26.5 „ | 6, or 17.6 „ |
| V. 2 (end) | 113 | 14, or 12.4 „ | 18, or 16 „ | 50, or 44.2 „ |
| Totals | 986 | 132, or 13.4 „ | 166, or 16.8 „ | 258, or 26.2 „ |

[1] Taken from Stoll.

[2] If I understand Mr. Stoll rightly, under the head of rime he gives the ratio of *couplets* to total number of lines: I give ratio of riming lines to total. If this is correct, his figures for rime should be doubled in comparing them with mine. This would in no way modify the conclusions.

[3] *Satiro-mastix* omitted, because it is largely prose.

## Old Fortunatus.

| Scene | Lines of verse | Feminine endings | Run-on lines | Riming lines |
|---|---|---|---|---|
| I. 1 | 234 | 12, or 5.1% | | 80, or 34.2% |
| I. 2 | 75 | 9, or 12 „ | | 26, or 34.7 „ |
| I. 3 | 87 | 6, or 6.9 „ | | 36, or 41.4 „ |
| II. 1 | 123 | 12, or 9.8 „ | | 18, or 14.6 „ |
| II. 2 | 159 | 13, or 8.2 „ | | 58, or 36.5 „ |
| III. 1 | 216 | 25, or 11.6 „ | | 62, or 28.7 „ |
| III. 2 | 94 | 11, or 11.7 „ | | 34, or 36.2 „ |
| IV. 1 | 151 | 12, or 8 „ | | 60, or 39.7 „ |
| IV. 2 | 54 | 2, or 3.7 „ | | 18, or 33.3 „ |
| V. 1 | 136 | 11, or 8.1 „ | | 62, or 45.6 „ |
| V. 2 | 280 | 26, or 9.3 „ | | 112, or 40 „ |
| *Totals* | 1609 | 139, or 8.6 „ | | 566, or 35.2 „ |

## Whore of Babylon.

| Scene | Lines of verse | Feminine endings | Run-on lines | Riming lines |
|---|---|---|---|---|
| I | 251 | 47, or 18.7% | | 18, or 7.2% |
| II | 285 | 23, or 8.1 „ | | 146, or 51.2 „ |
| III | 192 | 38, or 19.8 „ | | 62, or 32.3 „ |
| IV | 180 | 33, or 18.3 „ | | 36, or 20 „ |
| V | 265 | 52, or 19.6 „ | | 40, or 15.1 „ |
| VI | 160 | 59, or 36.9 „ | | 6, or 3.8 „ |
| VIII | 174 | 32, or 18.4 „ | | 38, or 21.8 „ |
| IX | 168 | 23, or 13,7 „ | | 62, or 36.9 „ |
| X | 305 | 42, or 13.7 „ | | 76, or 24.9 „ |
| XII | 92 | 8, or 8.7 „ | | 54, or 58.7 „ |
| XIII | 50 | 7, or 14 „ | | 16, or 32 „ |
| *Totals* | 2122 | 364, or 17.1 „ | | 554, or 26.1 „ |

A glance at the statistics for run-on lines in Webster, *Sir Thomas Wyatt*, and *The Honest Whore* shows that this test is absolutely noncommittal. Every scene in *Sir*

*Thomas Wyatt*, allowing for the inadequate length of the extract in XIII, is just about what we find in Dekker's play.

In the matter of feminine endings, the three plays of Dekker show a remarkable variation for so short a space of time. Since the general average of the *Whore of Babylon*,[1] however, is 17.1%, and since six separate scenes in it have an average of over 18%, it is obviously quite possible that Dekker might have written a scene in *Sir Thomas Wyatt* which has an average of 20%, especially when such a scene is short, and a single chance disyllable at the end of a line might raise the average of the whole scene two points. In Webster's plays, on the other hand, the *Cure for a Cuckold*,[1] as an entire play, has an average just under 20%. But the *Cure for a Cuckold* was separated from *Sir Thomas Wyatt* by a gap of many years. *The White Devil* and *The Duchess of Malfi*, which are much nearer in time, and consequently more in point, have averages so high that the highest scenes in *Sir Thomas Wyatt* seem less like Webster than like Dekker. On the whole, then, we may say that a percentage of 20 in feminine endings creates a slight presumption in favor of Webster; but it is very slight, and is practically reduced to zero in scenes I, III, and VIII, by the fact that it disagrees there with the other metrical tests which are strongly in favor of Dekker.

The rime-test is more decisive. In *Sir Thomas Wyatt* there are four scenes which have riming averages of

---

[1] It will be remembered that neither *The Whore of Babylon* nor the *Cure for a Cuckold* is of wholly undisputed authorship. If we lay these aside in discussing feminine endings, Webster's average in his other plays will be as much above 20% as Dekker's is below that mark throughout.

13% or below, while all the other scenes in the play—with the exception of XIII, which is a mere fragment—are well above 20%. Now in the three plays of Dekker's analyzed above, out of a total of thirty-two scenes—excluding *Honest Whore* III. 2, which is only 19 lines long—there are only seven scenes which have averages below 20%, and only three which have averages below 13%.[1] This is not positive proof: Dekker might have written the low scenes in *Wyatt*; but it creates a presumption in favor of Webster. Again, we are certain that Webster had some share in this play, and we know that in his later plays he never has a rime-average of 20%. Consequently, we cannot give Webster any of the other scenes without supposing that he used rime now as he never did later. Such a supposition is possible, since Webster was then in his formative stage; but it seems rather improbable. We are willing to give him some scenes with comparatively few feminine endings, because there are no other scenes, and he must have some share in the play; but when we find certain scenes with the low rime-average of Webster's extant work, and other scenes with the high average common in Dekker, the presumption certainly is that they should be divided accordingly. This would give to Webster Scenes II, VI, X, and XIV, and in doing so would agree with the word-test, since all of these are scenes with high word-averages.

There are one or two other peculiarities of Dekker's rime which are worth noting. He frequently uses the rime of a short, imperfect line with a long one, or

---

[1] This same continuous high average in rime is found throughout Dekker's other plays also, although I have not troubled the reader with the exact figures.

riming couplets in which one line has a pronounced
break just before the rime; and he is also fond of rime
between the last line of one speech and the first line of
the next. Webster very seldom uses any of these,
although isolated specimens of all three can be found
in his works. Now tricks of rime like this could not
be attributed to Webster on the ground that he was
a beginner; they are matters, not of age, but of
idiosyncrasy. Consequently, these are valuable evidence. In looking over the table of these rime-tests,
we must not lay too much stress on one or two
instances, because, in the first place, Webster does
use them occasionally, and, in the second place, one
or two of them might, like one or two parallel passages,
simply represent a touch of Dekker's pen in revising.
When, however, we find an unusual number of these
peculiarities in a scene, we may consider it specially
strong evidence of Dekker's work. Such is the case in
Scenes VIII, XV, XVI, XVII, and perhaps also I and IV.

Now it will be noticed that in VIII, XV, XVII,
I, and IV, these metrical criteria agree perfectly with
the word-test; but that in XVI they, and the general
rime-test also, defy it point blank. As a matter of
fact, we shall find other tests disagreeing about XVI.
It is a peculiar scene, and one which can only be
explained, I think, by assuming collaboration between
the authors. We will discuss this more at length
separately.

Putting aside scene XVI then for the present,
we find that the word-test and the metrical tests agree
in giving Webster II, VI, X, and probably XIV,
although the word-average here is only .286. The
metrical tests and word-test agree in giving Dekker
VIII, XV, XVII, and I and IV, although the metrical
evidence is not so strong in the last two. Scene V

is a very short scene, and its brevity makes all tests applied to it uncertain. Its high word-average points to Webster, while the rime in it would suggest Dekker, but would not be absolutely impossible for Webster. In all the other scenes the low word-average receives some support from the high percentage of rime; and the two together point strongly, but hardly conclusively, to Dekker.

So much for metrical tests. Now under the parallel-passage and incident-tests there is so little material that I shall not attempt to take them up separately; but instead will go through the play scene by scene, saying everything that can be said about each scene as it comes.

Scene I. There is one parallel passage from Dekker:

*Wyatt* I:

>    Our ocean shall his petty brooks devour.

*Wonder of a Kingdom* II:

>                              Be not the sea,
>    To drink strange rivers up, yet still be dry.

*Whore of Babylon*, p. 231:

>    You see what ocean can replenish you,
>    Be you but duteous, tributary streams.

The following quotation from Stoll, containing a long extract from this scene, is also in point here:

Wyatt[1] speaks with an abrupt force, a dogged reiteration, and a breeziness very like Dekker.

>    I'll damn my soul for no man, no, for no man.
>    Who at doomsday must answer for my sin?
>    Not you, nor you, my lords.
>    Who named Queen Jane in noble Henry's days?
>    Which of you all durst once displace his issue?
>    My lords, my lords, you whet your knives so sharp

---

[1] *John Webster*, p. 50.

> To carve your meat,
> That they will cut your fingers.
> The strength is weakness that you build upon.
> The King is sick,—God mend him, ay, God
>                 mend him!—
> But were his soul from his pale body free,
> Adieu, my lords, the court no court for me!

That is certainly not Webster's hand, and certainly is Dekker's. Parallels in Dekker are abundant; a short search yields these:

> TERRILL. If she should prove mankind, 'twere rare—fie, fie,
>   See how I lose myself amongst my thoughts,
>   Thinking to find myself; my oath, my oath.
> SIR QUIN. I swear another, let me see by what,
>   By my long stocking and my narrow skirts,
>   Not made to sit upon, she shall to court.
>   I have a trick, a charm, that shall lay down
>   The spirit of lust, and keep thee undeflowered;
>   Thy husband's honour saved, and the hot King,
>   Shall have enough, too. Come, a trick, a charm.
>                   *Sat.* p. 225.[1]
> CANDIDO. My gown, George, go, my gown.—A happy land,
>   Where grave men meet each cause to understand.
>   . . . . . . . . . . . . . . . . . .
>   Come, where 's the gown?
>   . . . . . . . . . . . . . . . . . .
>   Good wife, kind wife, it is a needful trouble, but for
>                 my gown!
>                 *H. W.* p. 139.[2]
> GEORGE. Do 't; away, do 't.      Ib. p. 135.
> LODOVICO. Do, do, bravely.      Ib. p. 222.
> TUCCA. Crispinus shall do 't, thou shalt do 't, heir apparent
>   of Helicon, thou shalt do 't.   *Sat.* p. 210.

Here there is the same liveliness, boisterousness, downrightness of manner, and—what is equally significant—the same style and rhythm.

[1] Dekker's Works.         [2] Mermaid Ed.

Scene II. The high word-average and low rime-average of this scene are supported by three parallel passages from Webster:

(a) *Wyatt* II:

> The flattering bells that shrilly sound
> At the king's funeral.

*White Devil* III. 2:

> What are whores!
> They are those flattering bells have all one tune,
> At weddings and at funerals.

(b) *Wyatt* II:

> Who would wear fetters,
> Though they were all of gold, or to be sick,
> Though his faint brows for a wearing night-cap
> Wore a crown?

*Duchess of Malfi* IV. 2:

> What would it pleasure me to have my throat cut
> With diamonds? or to be smotheréd
> With cassia? or to be shot to death with pearls?

(c) *Wyatt* II:

GUILD. The Tower will be a place of ample state:
> Some lodgings in it will, like dead men's skulls,
> Remember us of frailty.

JANE. We are led
> With pomp to prison. O prophetic soul!
> Lo, we ascend into our chairs of state
> Like several coffins, in some funeral pomp,
> Descending to their graves.

*Monumental Column*:

> Thy foundation doth betray
> Thy frailty, being builded on such clay.
> This shows the all-controlling power of fate,
> That all our sceptres and our chairs of state
> Are but glass-metal, that we are full of spots,
> And that, like new-writ copies, to avoid blots,
> Dust must be thrown upon us.

*White Devil* IV. 1 :

> You speak as if a man
> Should know what fowl is coffined in a baked meat
> Afore you cut it open.

The following extracts from both Webster and Dekker should also be mentioned here. I do not think that they give Dekker a counter claim to the above passage, because, in the first place, they parallel only one phrase, whereas the *Monumental Column* runs parallel to the whole thought; and, secondly, because the passage from Dekker which is closest in wording—the one from *Satiro-mastix*—is wholly different in tone, being facetious instead of serious. Nevertheless, the following passages show the danger of assigning speeches recklessly to Webster, simply because they mention a dead man's skull. Possibly they may also show the influence of one of these poets on the other.

(1) Webster's *Duchess of Malfi* III. 5 :

> Your kiss is colder
> Than that I have seen an holy anchorite
> Give to a dead man's skull.

*White Devil* V. 4 :

> O, fatal! he throws earth upon me!
> A dead man's skull beneath the roots of flowers.[1]

Dekker's *Satiro-mastix*,[2] p. 238 :

> If a bare head (being like a dead man's skull)
> Should bear up no praise else but this, it sets
> Our end before our eyes.

---

[1] Notice that here the vision of the skull does 'remember' Flamineo 'of frailty'.

[2] *Satiro-mastix* was published in 1602, the same year in which Henslowe mentions *Lady Jane*, which was probably the same play as *Sir Thomas Wyatt*. So we cannot tell which passage was written first.

*Phoenix*, p. 96: Sithence then that worms must be our last companions, and that the pillows upon which we are to rest for ever are within but dead men's skulls, whereof should we be proud?

*Honest Whore I* II. 1:

> Though his face
> Look uglier than a dead man's skull.

Stoll quotes passage (c) above, and also the second line of this scene,

> Alas! how small an urn contains a king!

as the only things in the whole play which seemed to him especially suggestive of Webster. On the whole, whether Dekker had any hand in this scene or not, it seems practically certain that Webster wrote most of it.

Scenes III and IV. For these two scenes I have no additional evidence.

Scene V. The shortness of this scene makes both the word-test and the metrical tests rather uncertain. However, it is very closely connected in incident with the following scene, as this shows the flight of the treasurer, and the next scene opens with the treasurer seeking pardon, while these are the only two scenes in which the treasurer appears. As the next scene is probably Webster's, this would naturally go with it. There is one very Dekkerian peculiarity of rime:

TREASURER. Is my horse ready?
PORTER.                                It is, my lord,
TREASURER. Then will I fly this fearful council board.

but this might simply mean that the scene was retouched. No very certain conclusions can be drawn.

Scene VI. The only additional evidence to support Webster's authorship in this scene is the character of Wyatt. His speeches here seem more argumentative, colorless, and trite than in the Dekker scenes. It is nothing very pronounced, however, and may be merely a matter of personal impression. As the scene is 89 solid lines long, the high word-test and low rime-test together seem strong evidence for Webster, even without other support.

Scene VII. The atmosphere of this scene is certainly that of Dekker's low-life studies. Brett, the clown, and the market girl with her eggs, are just such sketches as we get in *The Shoemaker's Holiday* and similar plays. This, with the low word-average and four riming couplets in only 13 lines of verse, points strongly to Dekker.

Scene VIII. Stoll quotes the following passage from this scene as especially typical of Dekker:

> O, at the general sessions, when all souls
> Stand at the bar of justice, and hold
> Their new-immortalizèd hands, O then
> Let the remembrance of their tragic ends
> Be razed out of the bead-roll of my sins!

He says of this and similar passages:

For in these there is a sweet personal tone—one that Webster never shows, and had he ever had, he could hardly have so outlived,—that is altogether like that of the creator of Jane [in *Shoemaker's Holiday*] Bellafront, and Orlando Friscobaldo.

The following parallel passage between this scene and Scene VI should also be noticed here. Just what it indicates is uncertain. Scene VIII must be largely by Dekker, and Scene VI must be partly at least by Webster.

*Wyatt* VIII:

> Amen; I bear a part;
> Ay, with my tongue,—I do not with my heart.

VI. p. 188:

> Yet have I borne a part,
> Laying the commons' troubles next my heart.

p. 189:

> O, let mine eyes,
> In naming that sweet youth observe their part,
> Pouring down tears sent from my swelling heart.

Stoll thinks that these sound like Dekker, and it is true that the rime of a full line with a fragment of another is much more common in Dekker, although it is not—as Stoll seems to imply—wholly unknown in Webster.

Scene IX. The low word-average and high rime-percentage here are supported by the following passages from Dekker:

(a) *Wyatt* IX:

> God pardon thee,
> And lay not to thy soul this grievous sin!
> Farewell; and when thou spend'st this ill-got gold,
> Remember how thy master's life was sold:
> Thy lord that gave thee lordships, made thee great,
> Yet thou betray'd'st him as he sat at meat.

*Virgin Martyr* IV. 2:[1]

DOR. You two, whom I like fostered children fed,
And lengthened out your starvèd life with bread;
You be my hangmen! whom, when up the ladder
Death haled you to be strangled, I fetched down,
Clothed you, and warmed you, you two my tormentors!
BOTH. Yes, we.
DOR. Divine Powers pardon you!

(b) *Wyatt* IX: O God, O God, that ever I was born!
*Roaring Girl* IV. 2: O God, O God, feed at reversion now? [?]

(c) *Wyatt* IX: O, colon cries out most tyrannically!

---

[1] The authorship of this scene is uncertain as yet, but it sounds like Dekker throughout.

*Virgin Martyr* III. 3:[1] And curse my feet for not ambling up and down to feed colon.

Stoll speaks of a Dutch phrase in the last speech, by which I suppose he means 'rustic and lustic.' This would, of course, point to Dekker.

Finally there is some likeness of incident between this scene and *The Virgin Martyr*. Here a low servant, who has been kindly treated by his master, betrays him for money, is reproached as shown in passage (a), and hangs himself in remorse. In *The Virgin Martyr* two servants who have been kindly used by their mistress, Dorothea, act as her tormentors for money, are reproached by her as shown in passage (a), and then are led out and hanged by the officers of the law.

Scene X. There is one marked parallel passage from Webster :

*Wyatt* X :

> The fox is subtle, and his head once in,
> The slender body easily will follow.

*White Devil* III. 2 :

> He that does all by strength, his wit is shallow :
> Where a man's head goes through, each limb will follow.

There is also one little detail of incident, which, though not strong, may point to Webster. Queen Mary speaks here of Philip's picture, and the impression which it makes on her. Pictures play an important part in Webster's plays. In *The White Devil*, Isabella is accustomed to steal out nightly to kiss the painting of her husband, and she is poisoned by an ointment smeared over it. In *The Devil's Law Case* III. 1, Leonora gazes at a picture and receives an evil inspiration from it; and again in IV. 2, Crispiano's picture is brought into court and shown as

---

[1] This scene has been generally assigned to Dekker.

evidence.[1]    I cannot find anything like this in Dekker,
nor is there any mention of a picture of Philip in
Holinshed's *Chronicle*, the source of *Wyatt*.

These things, together with the very high word-
average, the very low rime-average, and the unusual
length of the scene, which makes both of these tests
more reliable, make it certain that Webster wrote
part of this scene, and probable that he wrote nearly
all of it.

Scene XI.    At first sight, the account of Jane's
dream here sounds a little like that of the Duchess of
Malfi, told in III. 5 of that play.    Stoll, however, very
justly says that this is simply part of the traditional
machinery in this type of play, repeated frequently
in earlier plays,[2] and therefore meaning practically
nothing as to authorship.    The moderate word-average
and high rime-average point to Dekker, and there
seems to be nothing to contradict this assumption.
The general tone is certainly that of Dekker.    Take,
for example, the closing lines:

GUILD.    Entreat not, Jane: though she our bodies part,
        Our souls shall meet: farewell, my love!
JANE.                        My Dudley, my own heart!

This is, in a cruder form, the simple pathos of Bellafront in *The Honest Whore*, and of Jane in *The Shoemaker's Holiday*.

Scene XII.    The evidence of the word-test and
metrical tests is supported by the following parallel
passages from Dekker:

[1] Also Contarino asks Leonora for her picture, by which he
means her daughter, *Devil's Law Case* I. 1.
[2] Stoll mentions these: *Richard III* I. 4; v. 3; Duke Humphrey's
and his wife's dreams in *Contention*, pp. 421–422; *Henry VI* II I. 2;
*Sir Thomas More*, Dyce ed., p. 75.

(a) *Wyatt* XII:

> Fight valiantly, and by the Mary God,
> You that have all your lifetime silver lacked
> Shall get new crowns,—marry, they must be cracked.

*Shoemaker's Holiday* I. 1 : Crack me the crowns of the French knaves; a pox on them, crack them; fight, by the Lord of Ludgate; fight, my fine boy.

(b) *Wyatt* XII [speaking of Sir George Harper]:

> Henceforth, all harpers for his sake shall stand,
> But for plain ninepence throughout all the land.

*The Peace is Broken*, p. 160 [Petition of vintners to the Empress Money]: May it therefore please thee ... to send at least some of thy harpers to sound their nine-penny music in our ears.

(c) *Wyatt* XII: He shall pass and repass, juggle the best he can.

*Shoemaker's Holiday* IV. 5: For they mean to fall to their hey-pass and repass, pindy pandy, which hand will you have, very early.  [?]

The following passage is quoted from this scene by Stoll as very typical of Dekker. The remarks which he makes on the extract already cited in Scene I were applied to this also. For these, and somewhat parallel citations from Dekker's works, see the discussion of that scene.

WYATT. He shall pass and repass, juggle the best he can.
         Lead him into the city.  Norry, set forth,
         Set forth thy brazen throat, and call all Rochester
         About thee; do thy office; fill
         Their light heads with proclamations, do;
         Catch fools with lime-twigs dipt with pardons.
         But Sir George, and good Sir Harry Isley,
         If this gallant open his mouth too wide,
         Powder the varlet, pistol him, fire the roof
         That's o'er his mouth.

He craves the law of arms, and he shall ha 't:
Teach him our law, to cut 's throat if he prate.
If louder reach thy proclamation,
The Lord have mercy upon thee!

NORRY. Sir Thomas, I must do my office.

HARP. Come, we'll do ours, too.

WYATT. Ay, ay, do, blow thyself hence.
Whoreson, proud herald, because he can
Give arms, he thinks to cut us off by th' elbows.
Masters, and fellow soldiers, say will you leave
Old Tom Wyatt?

(This scene as a whole is clearly Dekker's.)

Scene XIII. There are two parallel passages from Dekker:

(a) *Wyatt* XIII: If you give an inch he 'll take an ell; if you give an ell he'll take an inch.

*Honest Whore II* II. 2: If you give your wife a yard she 'll take an ell. ... For, if you take a yard, I 'll take an ell. [*]

(b) *Wyatt* XIII [Brett's address to his men]: My fine, spruce, dapper, finical fellows.

*Shoemaker's Holiday* III. 1: Stay, my fine knaves, you arms of my trade, you pillars of my profession.[1]

III. 4: Now, my true Trojans, my fine Firk, my dapper Hodge, my honest Hans,[1] etc.

Like Dekker, too, and unlike Webster, are the jokes of Brett and the clown, the use of such slang or nonsense words as ' Camocho,' ' Calimanco,' and the reference to Dondego's and Paul's cathedral. This, combined with the decidedly low word-average, clearly shows this scene to be Dekker's.

Scene XIV. This is an uncertain scene. The word-average is .286, which rather favors Webster, but is not impossible for Dekker, especially in so short

---

[1] Pointed out by Stoll.

a scene. Every single metrical test that can be applied favors Webster; but these are not so conclusive as they would be in a longer extract. It will be noticed that, although Brett and the clown are on the stage, they say almost nothing. This looks as if the author of the scene did not feel at home with such characters. On the whole, the evidence favors Webster, but is decidedly inconclusive.

Scene XV. A word-average of .036, a rime-average of 43.3%, and the support of every other metrical test, would seem to give this plainly to Dekker, in spite of its brevity and lack of supporting evidence.

Scene XVI. There are two parallel passages for this scene, a fairly good one from Webster, and a strong one from Dekker:

*Webster:*

*Wyatt* XVI:[1]

> And will you count such forcement treachery?
> Then make the silver Thames as black as Styx,
> Because it was constrain'd to bear the barks
> Whose battering ordnance should have been employ'd
> Against the hinderers of our royalty.

*White Devil* III. 1:

> Condemn you me for that the duke did love me!
> So may you blame some fair and crystal river
> For that some melancholic distracted man
> Hath drowned himself in 't.

*Dekker.*

*Wyatt* XVI:

> Great men, like great flies, through laws' cobwebs
>                                                 break,
> But the thinn'st frame the prison of the weak.  [*]

---

[1] I found out afterward that Mr. Stoll had already noticed this parallelism.

*The Devil is in It*, p. 287 :

JOVINELLI.        You must hang up the laws.
OCTAVIO.    Like cobwebs in foul rooms, through which
                                          great flies
              Break through, the less being caught by the
                                          wing there dies.[1]

*Match Me in London* IV :

You oft call Parliaments and there enact
Laws good and wholesome, such as whoso break
Are hung by th' purse or neck, but as the weak
And smaller flies i' the spider's web are ta'en,
When great ones tear the web and free remain.

*Whore of Babylon*, p. 231 :

                    Home we 'll therefore send
These busy working spiders . . . let them there
Weave in their politic looms nets to catch flies.

Notice that the passage from *Match Me in London* uses the very same rimes, ' break ' and ' weak,' as are used in *Wyatt*.

Now, what are we to say about this scene? The word-average in it, .458, is very high, very strong for Webster; the metrical tests are very strong for Dekker, and we have passages from both. If we analyze the scene, we shall find some things rather peculiar about the metrical details. All the traces of Dekker seem to be bunched together in three passages, aggregating only about 40% of the verse-part of the scene, and the second of these contains the parallel passage from Dekker given above, while the parallel passage from Webster is not included in any of these. Leaving out the prose part, this is the way the scene divides up :

Lines   1–40, no rime.
    „    41–54, 6 couplets.

[1] The first of these parallels, the one from *The Devil is in It*, was pointed out by Dyce. The others have not before been noticed.

Lines   55–68, no rime.  This contains the parallel
               passage to Webster.
  „      69–99, 8 couplets. This contains the parallel
               passage to Dekker.
  „   100–116, no rime.
  „   117–122, 2 couplets.

Moreover, in the portions which are free from rime,
some of the lines have a powerful, rugged beat
accompanied with trisyllabic feet, which is not typical
of Dekker, and somewhat like the mature Webster.
Again, putting the riming lines by themselves, we
have 32 verse-lines, or about 27 solid lines, containing
only 6 trisyllabic Latin words, or an average of
about .200, while the average of the whole scene
is .458.

Of course, this slicing up of scenes has its dangers,
and we must not lay too much stress upon its
results; but nevertheless, when we compare these
facts with the high word-test, it certainly does look
as if Webster wrote the original scene, and Dekker
retouched certain parts of it.

Additional evidence of Webster's original authorship
is furnished by the incident-test. Holinshed's chronicle, the source of this play, gives no description of
the trial of Lady Jane, merely stating in less than
a sentence that she was tried and taken back to
prison. True, there is on another page[1] quite a description of the Duke of Northumberland's trial, and
this has obviously furnished some suggestions for
Scene XVI, since he speaks similarly there of pleading
to the indictment, and of the partiality which condemns
him and spares his fellow-offenders; but the fact
remains that there was nothing in Holinshed which
rendered a trial-scene for Lady Jane necessary, or

       [1] Holinshed's *Chronicle* 4, 4, ed. of 1808.

even strongly suggested it. The idea of a trial-scene must have originated in a man who had a natural tendency to trial-scenes. Dekker emphatically was not such a man, for there is not a single court-scene in all his writings. Webster emphatically was such a man, for he has left us three court trial-scenes [1] in a total output of only four plays and part of another. Moreover, in every one of Webster's trial-scenes we find a large amount of short, sharp dialogue and personal recrimination between different people, such as would never be allowed in an actual trial. This is just what we find in the trial of Lady Jane.

To conclude, then, it is certain that both writers had a hand in this scene, and it seems probable that Webster wrote the original scene, and that Dekker retouched parts of it.

Scene XVII. This is clearly Dekker's. The metrical evidence of every kind is overwhelmingly in his favor, far more so than in any other scene in the play. This agrees perfectly with the low word-test. The general atmosphere and spirit of the scene throughout is also Dekker's. In addition to all this, we have some help from the incident and parallel-passage tests.

In *Match Me in London* IV, we have the same picture of an executioner begging pardon of his intended victim; and there is some similarity in wording as well as in action.

*Wyatt* XVII

WIN.    It is her headsman.
GUILD.                    And demands a pardon.
            Only of her for taking off her head?

---

[1] *White Devil* III. 1 ; *Devil's Law Case* IV. 2 ; *Appius and Virginia* IV. 1.

*Match Me in London* IV:

JOHN.                           'S death, what are these?
VALASCO.   Your executioners appointed by the king.
JOHN.      These my executioners,
           And you my overseer, why kneel they?
VALASCO.   To beg your pardon, for they fear their work
           Will never please you.

Again, in both this scene and *The Virgin Martyr*
IV. 3, we have a beautiful and innocent young woman
brought out to execution before her lover or husband;
and in each case the lover swoons away from excess
of emotion.   There is some likeness in spirit, though
hardly in phraseology, between the speeches of Jane
and Dorothea on these occasions.

*Wyatt* XVII:

JANE.  Off with these robes, O, tear them from my side!
       Such silken covers are the gilt of pride.
       Instead of gowns, my coverture be earth,
       My worldly death a new celestial birth!
                . . . . . . . . . . O God,
       How hardly can we shake off this world's pomp,
       That cleaves unto us like our body's skin!
       Yet thus, O God, shake off thy servant's sin!

*Virgin Martyr* IV. 3:[1]

DOROTHEA.                     Nothing but to blame
          Thy tardiness in sending me to rest;
          My peace is made with Heaven, to which my soul
          Begins to take her flight: strike, O! strike quickly;
          And, though you are unmoved to see my death,
          Hereafter, when my story shall be read,
          As they were present now, the hearers shall
          Say of this Dorothea, with wet eyes,
          'She lived a virgin, and a virgin dies.'

───────

[1] I believe critics have not been unanimous as to the authorship of this scene; but the very similarities given above would
help to prove it Dekker's.

*Conclusion for Sir Thomas Wyatt.* In the light of what has been said, it seems probable that Webster wrote most of Scenes II, V, VI, X, XIV, and XVI, although some of these scenes were certainly retouched by Dekker, and all of them may have been. The rest of the play is almost certainly Dekker's. This would give Webster something like a third of the whole play, a much larger share than he had in either of the citizen comedies.

The above division is made on the assumption that Webster and Dekker were the only men concerned in this play. As a matter of fact, although this is the testimony of the title-page, it is not an absolute certainty. *Sir Thomas Wyatt* is generally supposed to be an abridgment of a play mentioned by Henslowe under the title of *Lady Jane.* Henslowe speaks of *Lady Jane* as being written in two parts, the second wholly the work of Dekker, and the first the joint production of Webster, Dekker, Heywood, Chettle, and Smith. Consequently, it is possible that passages from Chettle, Heywood, or Smith may be embodied in *Sir Thomas Wyatt.*[1] But it would be useless to discuss such questions as these at present, since no practical results could follow. We have offered such evidence as we possess on the shares of Dekker and Webster; and here we stop.

[1] The number of feminine endings in I, II, and VIII might indicate that the work of Dekker here was mixed with that of some other writer with a comparatively low word-average. Likewise Scene VI is a very colorless scene, with remarkably few feminine endings, and might be partly the work of any writer who had a high word-average. As shown already, however, these could be explained as the work of Dekker and Webster respectively.